Implementation of a Long-term Vegetation Monitoring Program at the Mississippi National River and Recreation Area

Natural Resource Report NPS/GLKN/NRTR—2012/616

Suzanne Sanders and Jessica Grochowski
National Park Service
Great Lakes Inventory and Monitoring Network
2800 Lake Shore Dr. East
Ashland, WI 54806

August 2012

U.S. Department of the Interior
National Park Service
Natural Resource Stewardship and Science
Fort Collins, Colorado

The National Park Service, Natural Resource Stewardship and Science office in Fort Collins, Colorado publishes a range of reports that address natural resource topics of interest and applicability to a broad audience in the National Park Service and others in natural resource management, including scientists, conservation and environmental constituencies, and the public.

The Natural Resource Technical Report Series is used to disseminate results of scientific studies in the physical, biological, and social sciences for both the advancement of science and the achievement of the National Park Service mission. The series provides contributors with a forum for displaying comprehensive data that are often deleted from journals because of page limitations.

All manuscripts in the series receive the appropriate level of peer review to ensure that the information is scientifically credible, technically accurate, appropriately written for the intended audience, and designed and published in a professional manner.

This report received formal peer review by subject-matter experts who were not directly involved in the collection, analysis, or reporting of the data, and whose background and expertise put them on par technically and scientifically with the authors of the information.

Views, statements, findings, conclusions, recommendations, and data in this report do not necessarily reflect views and policies of the National Park Service, U.S. Department of the Interior. Mention of trade names or commercial products does not constitute endorsement or recommendation for use by the U.S. Government.

This report is available from the Great Lakes Inventory and Monitoring Network (http://science.nature.nps.gov/im/units/glkn/index.cfm) and the Natural Resource Publications Management website (http://www.nature.nps.gov/publications/nrpm/).

Please cite this publication as:

NPS 607/116665, August 2012

Contents

Contents (continued)

Figures

Tables

Appendices

Executive Summary

We initiated a long-term vegetation monitoring program at the Mississippi National River and Recreation Area (MISS) in summer 2011. The goals of this monitoring program are to detect forest change and to draw inferences about forest health so that management recommendations can be provided to the park. We established 33 plots at MISS, distributed among four forest types: upland, cottonwood-box elder, green ash-box elder, and silver maple. Upland plots contained the greatest tree species diversity, with all common species regenerating. In the three riparian forest types, many species characteristic of these forests are not successfully regenerating and are now present only as large diameter individuals at very low densities. For example, in floodplain forests, we located no cottonwood individuals smaller than 15 cm in diameter at breast height (DBH), although most individuals were greater than 30 cm DBH. The lack of regeneration is a direct result of river impoundment, which moderates flooding and supplements low water flow. Floodplain species are dependent on high water events to scour surfaces and remove existing vegetation, creating germination sites.

Invasive species were evident in both upland and riparian sites. Two shrub taxa, buckthorn and exotic honeysuckles, were commonly observed in many upland plots. Both taxa were located in nine of the 10 total upland plots. In the plots where they were present, mean buckthorn cover was 14.4% and honeysuckle cover was 6.8%. In the 23 floodplain sites, garlic mustard was present at 10 of these sites and reed canarygrass at 13. Besides invasive plants, the invasive beetle, emerald ash borer, is now present in the Twin Cities metro area. This species disrupts the vascular system of all ash species, leading to tree death within about four years. In green ash-box elder forests, green ash comprised 39% of the density and 35% of the basal area. In upland plots, both green and black ash collectively represented 7% of the density and 6% of the basal area, while in cottonwood-box elder forests, ash represented 6% and 18% of the density and basal area, respectively.

Managers should make every effort to reduce the impacts of invasive plant species, particularly in areas where ash is abundant. The loss of ash trees will create gaps which can promote the establishment of buckthorn and honeysuckle. To address issues with regeneration, partial restoration of historic flow regimes, such as periodic drawdowns of water, can create suitable sites for germination and establishment of flood dependent species. Alternatively, managers may wish to consider restoration techniques that involve transplantation of two- and three-year-old saplings of these species. These plots will be revisited in 2017. Comparisons of change can be made at that time.

Acknowledgments

We are grateful for the vegetation monitoring field crew of Caitlin Clarke, Chris Groebner, Brian Pauley, Jaime Thibodeaux, and Alexandra Wardwell. Without their assistance, this project would in no way be possible. We are also indebted to Bill Route for boat transportation and to Tamberlain Jacobs and Nancy Duncan for planning and logistical assistance. We also wish to convey thanks to the natural resource staff at many of our partner parks. Finally, we have also greatly appreciated the assistance of Rebecca Key of the Great Lakes I&M Network for assistance with database development and refinement.

Introduction

Long-term forest monitoring provides an assessment of forest health by showing the status of plant communities at the time of each sampling event and elucidating how these communities change over time. Despite this value, large-scale monitoring programs for forest health with regularly scheduled return intervals are not common (for an exception, see U. S. Department of Agriculture (2005)).

In 2007, the National Park Service Great Lakes Inventory and Monitoring Network initiated a long-term forest vegetation monitoring program for nine national parks in the Great Lakes region. The general goals of this program are to monitor forest vegetation to gain a better understanding of its dynamics, and to compare, ultimately, vegetation indices to baseline conditions. The program was initiated at the Mississippi National River and Recreation Area (MISS) in the summer of 2011. As this was the first year of data collection at this park, no comparisons between time intervals can be made. Nonetheless, meaningful data were obtained to demonstrate the current status of MISS forests.

The goals of our long-term vegetation monitoring during the first sampling year at a given park focus on obtaining baseline data on the status of park forests. Here, we report on this effort at MISS. Specifically, we wanted to answer the following questions for key forest habitats: 1) What is the relationship between density and stem diameter for key tree species? 2) What is the basal area of both individual tree species and all species collectively? 3) What is the density of seedlings? 4) What is the percentage of shrub cover?

Methods

Sampling was conducted at MISS from 31 May–27 June, 2011. Sites were selected using a generalized random-tessellation stratified design (GRTS; Stevens and Olsen 2004), ensuring that sites were both randomly located and spatially balanced throughout the park. All sites were required to have a minimum of 10% forest cover. We checked all potential sites against an aerial photography layer in GIS prior to visiting them in the field. Potential sites that did not initially meet the minimum 10% forest cover requirement were moved the shortest distance possible, to a maximum of 100 m, so that they fell within the desired amount of cover. If a potential site could not be moved ≤100 m to meet the criteria, it was not sampled. Maps of individual sites are presented in Appendix A.

Field Methods

Basic Measurements

Sites were sampled using the Hybrid plot (Figure 1) developed specifically to meet the needs of our long-term monitoring program (Johnson et al. 2006, Johnson et al. 2008). The plot is composed of three 50 m parallel transects oriented east-west. Tree data were collected in a 6 m wide band along the length of each transect. Tree data collected included species, diameter at breast height (DBH), whether the tree was alive or dead, and any evident damage or disease. Trees were defined as having a DBH ≥2.5 cm. Groundlayer vegetation was collected in $1m^2$ quadrats placed every 5 m along each transect (n = 30 per plot). Within each quadrat, we

1

recorded all herbaceous, vine, and shrub species present as well as counted seedlings. Seedlings were defined as tree species <2.5 cm DBH, but at least 15 cm in height and showing evidence of growth from the previous year. Many species we commonly encountered reproduce vegetatively (e.g., aspen, basswood). Individual sprouts (i.e., both ramets and genets) were deemed "seedlings" if no aboveground connections between them, or a parent tree, were visible. Shrub cover was assessed within each of six 2.82 m radius (25 m^2 area) shrub circles, located at the transect ends. Here, we visually estimated percent cover of each shrub species present. We measured coarse woody materials (CWM) along each of the three transects using the planar intercept method (Brown 1974, (Woodall and Monleon 2007)). We recorded diameters at the point of intercept, the small end, and the large end; the length; the decay class (Woodall and Williams 205); and, if possible, the species. Because we defined CWM as having a diameter ≥7.5 cm (3 in), the length of a piece was measured only along the section where the diameter exceeded this amount. Finally, we performed a half-hour time-delimited search of the entire 50 m × 100 m plot area to locate any additional species not previously recorded in any of the sampling.

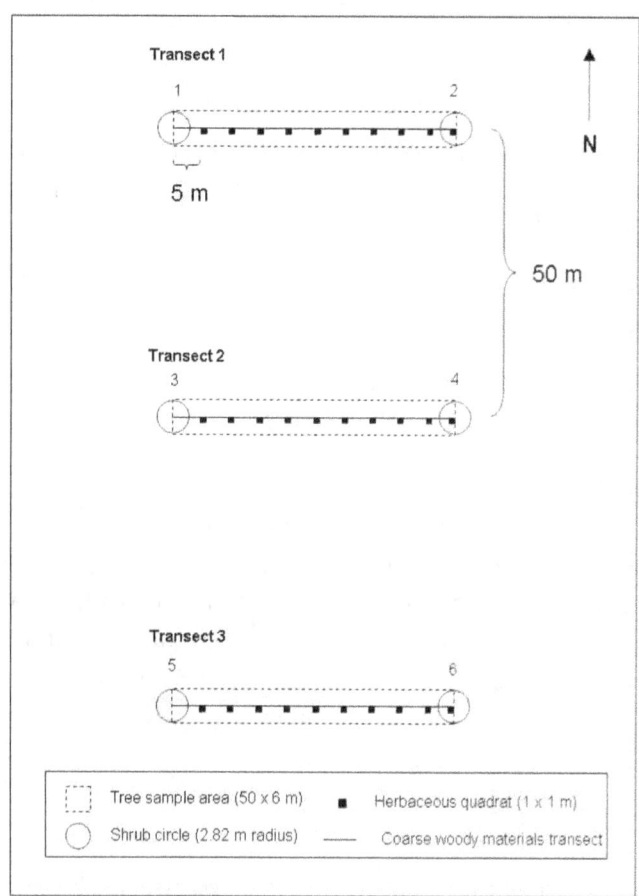

Figure 1. The Hybrid plot configuration consisted of three parallel transects, each 50 m long and oriented east-to-west.

Browse Assessments

We examined white-tailed deer (*Odocoileus virginianus* Zimm.) winter and summer browse pressure using two distinct measures. Direct browse is an assessment of visible browse, i.e., bites, directly evident on the plant. The direct browse measure is assessed on woody species. The indirect browse assessment is conducted on herbaceous species and does not focus on obvious, visible browse, but rather changes in herbs, only indirectly observed over time. These changes are typically manifested as fewer and smaller individuals of preferred herbaceous browse species.

Direct browse was measured along each of the three 50 m transects, and along the two 100 m transects running north-south between the east-west transects at the plot (broken down into 50 meter segments for consistency) (Figure 2). Direct browse measurements were conducted in 3.14 m^2 (1 m radius) circular sampling areas. These browse sampling circles were centered every 5 meters along each transect, for a total of 68 for each plot. This resulted in a total sampling area of 213 m^2. For each direct browse sampling circle, all woody species present in the browse zone, defined as the space between 0.20 m and 2.0 m in height, were recorded. In addition to species presence, evidence of any deer browse on that species in the sampling circle was recorded. Typically, winter browse surveys are conducted in the spring, prior to the new season's growth. Because we were not able to sample in the spring, we only considered a plant browsed when it was apparent that the browse occurred before the start of the current season's growth. This was evidenced by new growth arising from the bud immediately below the point of browse. Direct browse data were used to calculate a browse index equal to the ratio of woody species with evident browse to all woody species present (Morellet et al. 2001, Morellet et al. 2003).

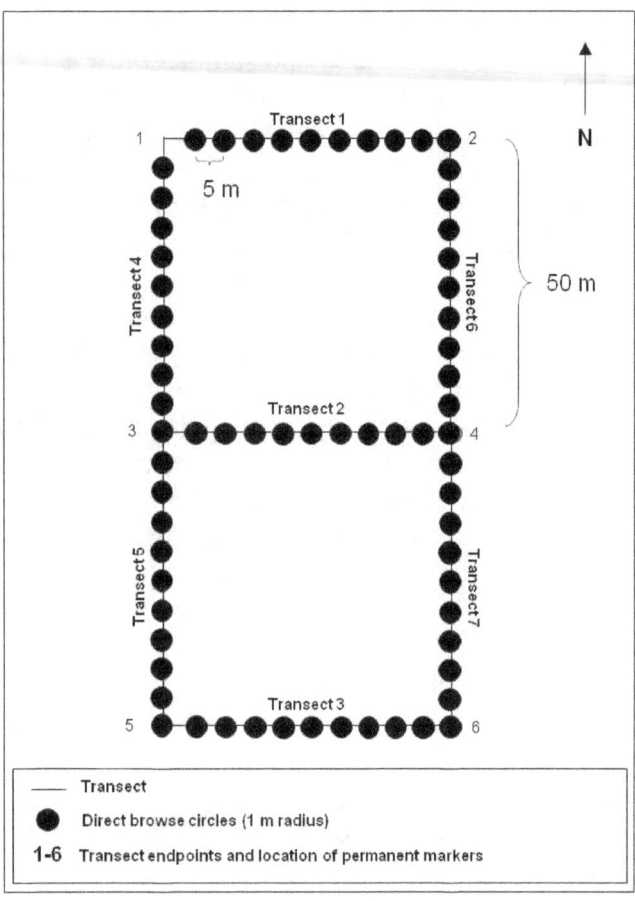

Figure 2. Direct browse sampling circles in a plot.

To assess the indirect impacts of summer browse on understory species, we selected three target species that are known to be browsed by white-tailed deer in the region: *Laportea canadensis* (L.) Weddell (wood nettle), *Osmorhiza* sp. Raf. (sweet cicely), and *Maianthemum racemosum* (L.) Link (false lily-of-the-valley). In each 1 m^2 herbaceous quadrat (see Figure 1), for each target species, we counted the number of individuals that were non-reproductive and unbrowsed, the number that were reproductive and unbrowsed, and the number that were browsed (regardless of reproductive state). We also measured the height of the tallest individual of each of the three target species, if present.

Tree Health

To assess tree health, we used an evidence-based approach whereby we examined each tree for the presence of broad classes of disease, damage, or injury (U.S. Department of Agriculture 2010). These classes included dieback, epicormic sprouting, wilted foliage, defoliation, discolored foliage, insect sign, and human induced stress. If a tree exhibited symptoms of one of these primary classes, a further classification of the damage or disease was made, based on predefined characteristics within each of the primary classes. For example, if a tree was classified as having discolored foliage, we would note whether this damage was in the form of (among other choices) marginal browning of the leaves, interveinal browning of the leaves, the leaves possessing a white coating, or a general yellowing of the leaves. This symptom-based assessment of damage and disease allows us to easily classify tree health issues, from which, a

4

symptom-based approach is more accurate than directly assigning a root cause to problems observed when at the field site. For some symptoms, there are dozens of possible causes and a pathologist or entomologist with specialization in the region would be needed to accurately assess the problem. Large-scale or persistent symptoms noted with this method can inform the park staff of potential disease or insect outbreaks, which would require further investigation by the park to identify the exact disease or pest.

Assigning Forest Types

Because we may want to stratify by forest or habitat type during later analyses (i.e., post stratification), we declared a forest type for all plots sampled. While we were present at the plot, we used the Minnesota Landcover Classification System (MLCCS, Leete and Richardson 1999) to declare a forest type.

Visual Assessment/Photo Points

Finally, documenting visual assessments of site change will be as important as statistical documentation, and potentially more informative. Therefore, we took six photographs at each plot. The six photo points were located at each of the six transect endpoints, with the camera facing into the plot (i.e., due east at points 1, 3, and 5 and due west at points 2, 4, and 6; see Figure 1).

Plant Identification

We attempted to identify all plants to the species level while in the field. When this was not possible, we typically collected specimens for later identification. In some instances, it was not possible to distinguish between multiple species present in a park, unless they were flowering or fruiting, which often was not the case. In these instances, we identified only to the genus level. Examples of this include *Pilea* Lindl. (false nettle), *Osmorhiza* (sweet cicely), and *Carex* L. (sedge). For *Amelanchier* sp., the genus was further subdivided into three groups of species complexes, with Group 1 containing *A. bartramiana*; Group 2 containing *A. arborea*, *A. laevis*, and *A. interior*; and Group 3 containing an uncertain number of species (Smith 2008). Finally, if a grass was not in flower or fruit, it was typically only possible to identify to the family (Poaceae) level. Finally, because we questioned the large occurrence of *Ulmus rubra* Muhl. (slippery elm) recorded in floodplain plots relative to *Ulmus americana* L. (American elm), we pooled data from these two species and are presenting it simply as *Ulmus* sp. L., or just elm.

Analysis and Classification Methods

Cluster Analysis

We felt that there was some degree of subjectivity required when using the MLCCS dichotomous key to assign forest types. Because multiple employees present at a site often assigned different types, we questioned the value of this data for our program. Further, the MLCCS recognizes subtle nuances in forests, such that this system tends to recognize more, rather than fewer, types. Our 33 plots were assigned to 12 different forest types. Grouping on these forest types would result in one to a few plots per type. For these reasons, we decided to use cluster analysis to place the 33 plots into groups with similar tree species composition. We limited inclusion in the cluster analysis to those species that were present in at least 8% (3 of 33) of the plots. Collectively, these plots supported 17 taxa meeting these criteria. The cluster analysis was based on the importance value, determined by the sum of the relative density and relative basal area of each species-plot combination (Dyer 2006, Elliott and Swank 2008). We used PC-ORD software with a Sørenson distance measure and a flexible beta linkage ($\beta = -0.25$, McCune and Grace 2002). Forest type names were assigned based on the dominant trees in these groups.

Functional Groups

All taxa were assigned to classes within each of four functional groups. Within the *life history group*, taxa were annual, biennial, or perennial. For taxa that are known to exhibit a range of life history strategies, we assigned the shortest strategy. For example, if a taxa is known to be either biennial or perennial, we assigned it to the biennial class. Within the *growth form group*, taxa were considered to be woody (trees and shrubs), graminoid (grasses, sedges, and rushes), or forbs. This latter class included ferns and fern allies in this report. For the *pollination group*, taxa were considered to be abiotically pollinated if the flowers are non-existent (conifers) or not showy, and not known to produce any sensory attractants. These are typically wind pollinated. Otherwise, taxa were considered to be biotically pollinated. Fern and fern allies were not assigned to classes within this functional group. Within the nativity group, taxa were assigned to either native, non-native, or native/non-native. Naturalized taxa were considered non-native. In some instances taxa were identified only to the genus level and could not be assigned a nativity group as species within these genera are both native and otherwise. One example of this is *Ranunculus* sp. (buttercup).

Coefficients of Conservatism

Coefficient of conservatism (COC) values describe the affinity of species to non-degraded habitats. Values range from zero (either non-native species or generalists with no faithfulness to any particular habitat) to 10 (conservative species found only in high-quality, non-degraded habitats). Since a given species may be conservative in one area of its distribution, but a generalist in the center of its range, COC values vary by region. Typically, values are assigned at the state level by experienced botanists and ecologists. For this report, we used COC values defined for the state of Wisconsin (Bernthal 2003). Although COC values have been assigned for wetland plant species in Minnesota (Milburn et al. 2007), there has been no comprehensive, statewide assignment of COC values for all plant species in Minnesota. Mean COC values were calculated for each of the four forest types.

Results

A total of 33 plots were completed at MISS (Figure 3). Thirty-eight tree species were recorded in the sampling plots (Appendix B), as were 35 shrub species, eight species of woody vines, and 167 herbaceous species. Cluster analysis, based on the importance values of the tree species present in each plot, revealed four distinct groups. We confirmed these groups using non-metric multidimensional scaling (NMS) and designated a forest type for each (Table 1): upland, cottonwood-box elder, green ash-box elder, and silver maple.

Table 1. Forest types at MISS and the plots classified in each.

Forest type	Plots
Upland	5002, 5006, 5018, 5031, 5033, 5039, 5073, 5082, 5096, 5097
Cottonwood-box elder	5004, 5016, 5020, 5022, 5038, 5056, 5076, 5084, 5099, 5148
Green ash-box elder	5010, 5021, 5034, 5042, 5052, 5104, 5140
Silver maple	5030, 5035, 5086, 5106, 5111, 5142

Upland Forests

The upland forest plots were near the uppermost reaches of the Riverway and between St. Paul and Hastings and exhibited a continuum of forest integrity. Plot ownership and locations include Anoka County Parks/Coon Rapids Dam Regional Park (5096), Ramsey County (5031), Macalester College/Ordway Nature Preserve (5039), Washington County/Lower Gray Cloud Island (5073), Dakota County Parks/Pine Bend Bluff State Natural Area (5082), Dakota County Parks/Spring Lake Park Reserve (5002, 5018), Dakota County Parks/Schaar's Bluff/Spring Lake Park Reserve (5097), the 3M corporation (5033), and the State of Minnesota/DNR land east of Hastings (5006).

Among the four forest types at MISS, this one had the greatest tree species richness with 24 species (Table 2). No single species was dominant in upland forests, but elm, bitternut hickory (*Carya cordiformis* (Wangenh.) K. Koch), and bur oak (*Quercus macrocarpa* Michx.) were both common and exhibited a range of size classes in this forest type (Table 2). All prominent species in upland forests appear to be regenerating, as is evidenced by greater densities in smaller size classes (Figure 4).

Seedling density varied highly by species but most of the prominent upland tree species had seedling densities greater than 800 seedlings/ha (Table 3). Exceptions to this were red oak (*Quercus rubra* L.) and basswood (*Tilia americana* L.) at 267 and 200 seedlings/ha, respectively (Table 3).

Twenty-seven shrub or woody vine species were identified (Table 4). Percent cover was less than one percent for all but three species: buckthorn (*Rhamnus cathartica* L., 12.95%), exotic honeysuckles (*Lonicera* ssp. L., 5.53%), and hairystem gooseberry (*Ribes hirtellum* Michx., 2.97%).

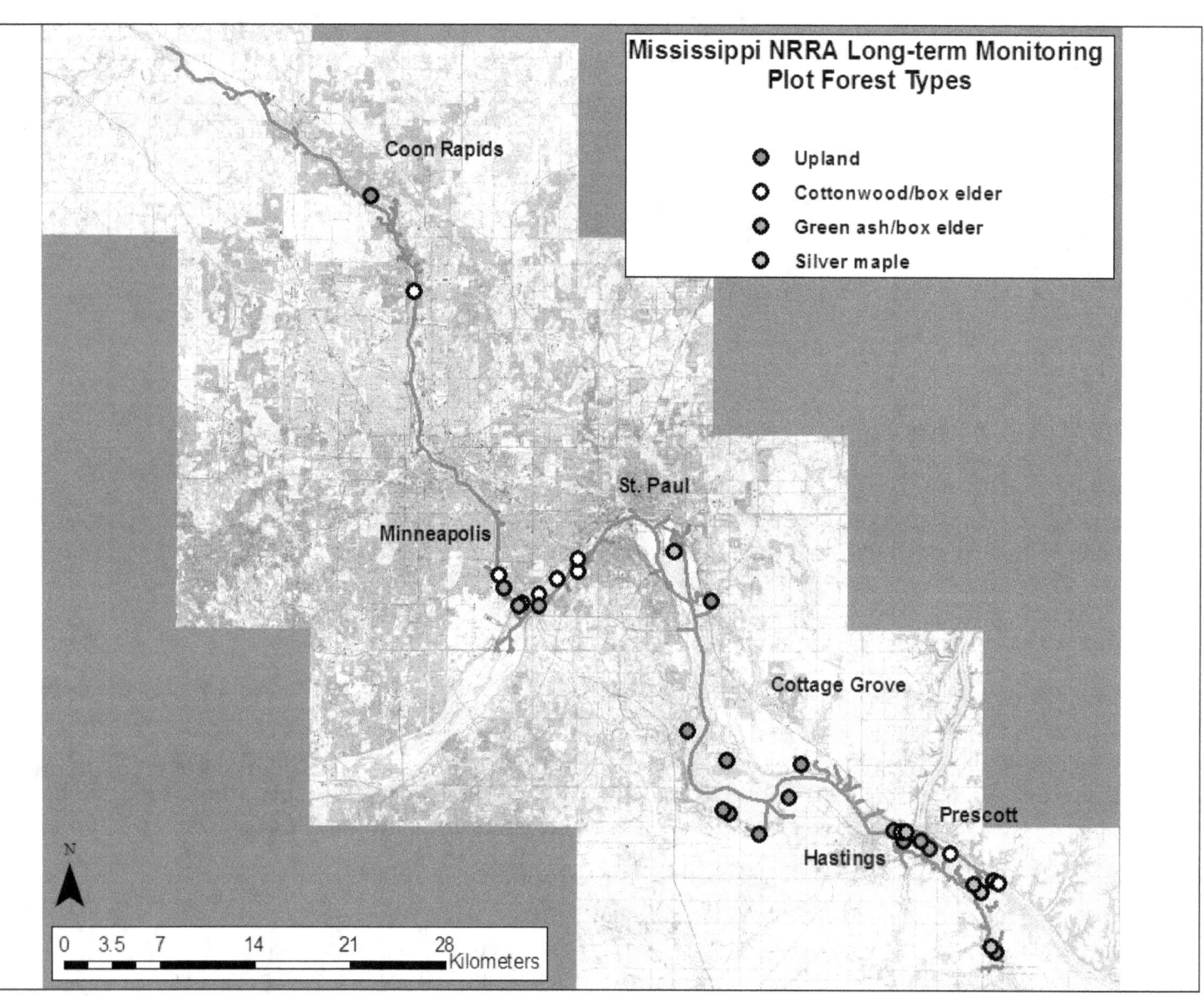

Figure 3. MISS long-term vegetation monitoring plot locations and forest types (in 2011).

Table 2. Basal area and density of live trees in upland forests at Mississippi NRRA, 2011.

Latin name	Common name	Basal area (m^2/ha)	Density (trees/ha)
Acer negundo	box elder	0.72	38.89
Acer nigrum	black maple	<0.01	1.11
Acer saccharum	sugar maple	0.08	6.67
Betula papyrifera	paper birch	0.74	30.00
Carya cordiformis	bitternut hickory	2.42	147.78
Celtis occidentalis	hackberry	1.02	104.44
Crataegus sp.	hawthorn	<0.01	1.11
Fraxinus nigra	black ash	0.06	18.89
Fraxinus pennsylvanica	green ash	1.21	41.11
Gymnocladus dioicus	Kentucky coffeetree	0.03	3.33
Juglans cinerea	butternut	0.03	1.11
Juniperus virginiana	eastern red cedar	0.14	15.56
Ostrya virginiana	ironwood	0.11	17.78
Populus deltoides ssp. *monilifera*	cottonwood	1.23	7.78
Populus tremuloides	trembling aspen	0.18	2.22
Prunus serotina	black cherry	1.27	42.22
Prunus virginiana	pin cherry	0.02	8.89
Quercus alba	white oak	1.24	6.67
Quercus ellipsoidalis	northern pin oak	1.24	5.56
Quercus macrocarpa	bur oak	5.60	47.78
Quercus rubra	red oak	1.76	47.78
Tilia americana	basswood	1.72	120.00
Ulmus sp.	American elm	2.20	170.00
Total		23.02	886.68

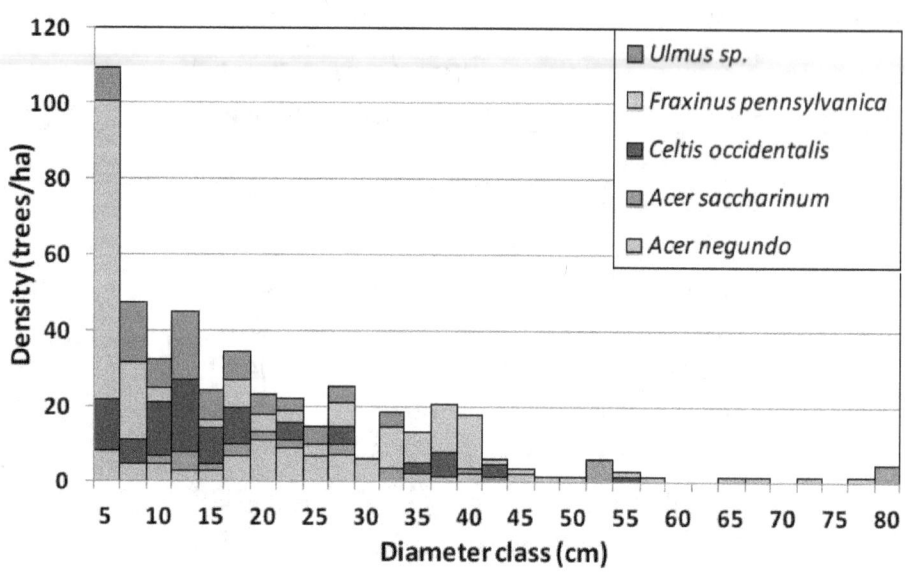

Figure 4. Densities and diameter classes of tree species in upland forests at Mississippi NRRA, 2011.

Table 3. Seedling density in upland forests at Mississippi NRRA, 2011.

Latin name	Common name	Density (seedlings/ha)
Acer negundo	box elder	400.00
Acer saccharum	sugar maple	100.00
Betula sp.	birch	66.67
Carya cordiformis	bitternut hickory	1,366.67
Celtis occidentalis	hackberry	2,133.33
Crataegus sp.	hawthorn	33.33
Fraxinus nigra	black ash	133.33
Fraxinus pennsylvanica	green ash	1,700.00
Gymnocladus dioicus	Kentucky coffeetree	100.00
Juniperus virginiana	eastern red cedar	66.67
Ostrya virginiana	ironwood	233.33
Populus tremuloides	trembling aspen	200.00
Prunus pensylvanica	pin cherry	200.00
Prunus serotina	black cherry	3,500.00
Prunus sp.	cherry	33.33
Prunus virginiana	chokecherry	2,333.33
Quercus ellipsoidalis	northern pin oak	66.67
Quercus rubra	red oak	266.67
Tilia americana	basswood	200.00
Ulmus sp.	elm	900.00
Total		14,033.33

Table 4. Shrub percent cover in upland forests at Mississippi NRRA, 2011.

Latin name	Common name	% Cover
Berberis vulgaris[1]	barberry	0.05
Cornus alternifolia	alternate-leaved dogwood	0.33
Cornus racemosa	gray dogwood	0.12
Corylus americana	American hazelnut	0.03
Euonymus atropurpurea	burningbush	0.08
Lonicera sp. (exotic)[1]	honeysuckle (exotic)	5.53
Lonicera morrowii[1]	Morrow's honeysuckle	0.55
Lonicera sp.[2]	honeysuckle	0.03
Menispermum canadense	moonseed	0.63
Parthenocissus sp.	Virginia creeper	2.42
Physocarpus opulifolius	ninebark	0.02
Rhamnus cathartica[1]	buckthorn	12.95
Ribes cynosbati	eastern prickly gooseberry	0.38
Ribes hirtellum	hairystem gooseberry	2.97
Ribes sp.	current/gooseberry	0.05
Rosa carolina	Carolina rose	0.02
Rubus idaeus ssp. *strigosus*	red raspberry	0.17
Rubus occidentalis	black raspberry	0.37
Rubus pensilvanicus	Pennsylvania blackberry	0.08
Rubus pubescens	dwarf red blackberry	0.20
Rubus setosus	setose blackberry	0.02
Sambucus nigra ssp. *canadensis*	black elderberry	0.03
Sambucus racemosa var. *racemosa*	red elderberry	0.40
Sambucus sp.	elderberry	0.03
Solanum dulcamara[1]	climbing nightshade	0.05
Smilax tamnoides	bristly greenbriar	0.32
Toxicodendron radicans	eastern poison ivy	0.18
Toxicodendron rydbergii	western poison ivy	0.05
Viburnum rafinesqueanum	downy arrowwood	0.02
Viburnum sp.	viburnum	0.02
Vitis riparia	riverbank grape	0.57
Zanthoxylum americanum	prickly ash	0.35

[1]non-native
[2]This genus contains both native and non-native species.

Cottonwood-Box Elder Forests

The cottonwood-box elder riparian forest type is typified by large diameter cottonwoods (*Populus deltoides* Bartram ex Marsh. ssp. *monilifera* (Aiton) Eckenwalder), with significant inclusions of box elder (*Acer negundo* L.) and silver maple (*Acer saccharinum* L.). Plot ownership and locations include Anoka County/Manomin County Park (5016), St. Paul Parks and Recreation Department/Hidden Falls Regional Park (5076), St. Paul Parks and Recreation Department/Crosby Farm Regional Park (5148, 5004), State of Minnesota/land east of Hastings (5022), Minnesota DNR/Pike Island (5056), Lilydale Regional Park/ St. Paul Parks and Recreation Department (5020, 5084), Minnesota DNR/Gores Pool Wildlife Management Area (WMA) (5038, 5099). Of these ten plots, seven were located within 5 km of the confluence of the Mississippi and Minnesota Rivers, three in the Gores Pool WMA downstream from Hastings, and one at Manomin County Park in Anoka County (Figure 3). Fifteen tree species were recorded in these plots, although one species, cottonwood, represented 45.0% of the basal area. Taxa with the greatest densities include box elder, silver maple, and elm (Table 5). Despite the large basal area, no cottonwood individuals with a diameter at breast height (DBH) were recorded smaller than 15 cm, and most individuals measured had a DBH >35 cm (Figure 5).

Table 5. Basal area and tree density in cottonwood-box elder forests at Mississippi NRRA, 2011.

Latin name	Common name	Basal area (m²/ha)	Density (trees/ha)
Acer negundo	box elder	4.22	150.00
Acer saccharinum	silver maple	9.61	133.70
Betula nigra	river birch	0.22	1.11
Celtis occidentalis	hackberry	0.48	39.26
Fraxinus nigra	black ash	0.15	21.11
Fraxinus pennsylvanica	green ash	1.84	79.88
Gleditsia triacanthos	honeylocust	0.03	1.11
Juglans cinerea	butternut	0.33	2.22
Juglans nigra	black walnut	0.02	4.94
Morus alba	white mulberry	0.03	1.23
Populus deltoides ssp. monilifera	cottonwood	15.12	51.48
Prunus virginiana	pin cherry	<0.01	1.11
Salix amygdaloides	peachleaf willow	0.28	1.11
Salix nigra	black willow	0.23	1.11
Ulmus sp.	elm	1.07	86.91
Total		33.63	576.28

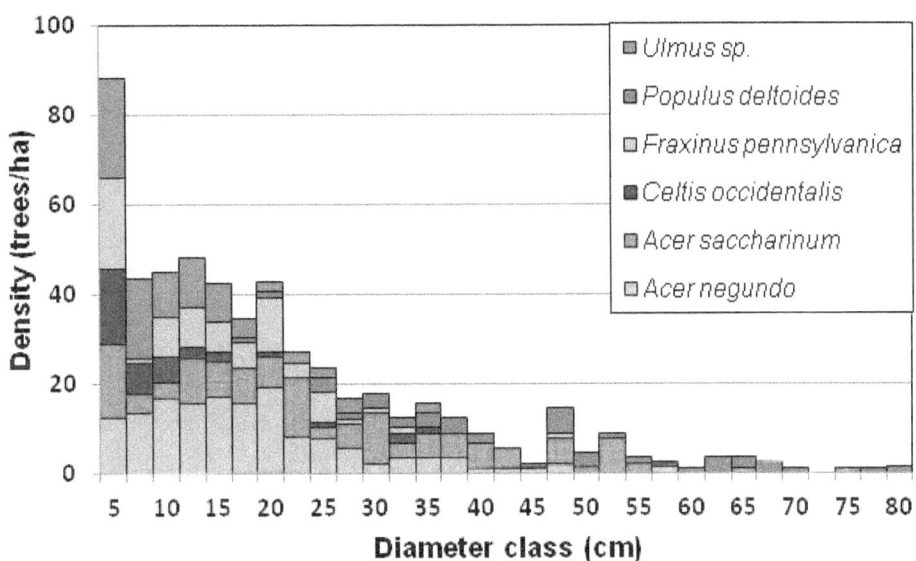

Figure 5. Densities and diameter classes of tree species in cottonwood-box elder forests at Mississippi NRRA, 2011.

Green ash was the most abundant species of seedlings in this forest type with 3,720 (Table 6) with black ash (*Fraxinus nigra* Marsh.), hackberry, and elm having greater than 900 seedlings/ha. Seedling density of silver maple, a foundation species in floodplain forests, was only 70.3 seedlings/ha. There were no cottonwood seedlings located in the plots in this forest type (Table 6).

Table 6. Seedling density in cottonwood-box elder forests at Mississippi NRRA, 2011.

Latin name	Common name	Density (seedlings/ha)
Acer negundo	box elder	566.67
Acer saccharinum	silver maple	70.37
Celtis occidentalis	hackberry	1,329.63
Fraxinus nigra	black ash	1,533.33
Fraxinus pennsylvanica	green ash	3,719.98
Prunus serotina	black cherry	33.33
Prunus virginiana	choke cherry	433.33
Tilia americana	basswood	66.67
Ulmus sp.	elm	966.67
Total		8,719.98

Shrub and woody vine occurrence in cottonwood-box elder forests was generally low and only four species showed greater than 1% cover: buckthorn (3.13%), Virginia creeper (*Parthenocissus* sp. Planch., 2.03%), riverbank grape *Vitis riparia* Michx. (a woody vine with 1.55% cover), and hairystem gooseberry (1.15%, Table 7). Including buckthorn, four non-native shrub taxa were recorded.

Table 7. Shrub percent cover in cottonwood-box elder forests at Mississippi NRRA, 2011.

Latin name	Common name	% Cover
Acer ginnala[1]	Amur maple	0.03
Cornus sericea	redosier dogwood	0.48
Euonymus atropurpurea	burning bush	0.03
Humulus lupulus	common hops	0.02
Lonicera sp. (exotic)[1]	honeysuckle (exotic)	0.15
Menispermum canadense	moonseed	0.12
Parthenocissus sp.	Virginia creeper	2.03
Physocarpus opulifolius	ninebark	0.02
Rhamnus cathartica[1]	buckthorn	3.13
Ribes americanum	American black current	0.42
Ribes hirtellum	hairystem gooseberry	1.15
Rubus idaeus ssp. strigosus	red raspberry	0.02
Rubus occidentalis	black raspberry	0.75
Rubus pubescens	dward red blackberry	0.05
Sambucus nigra ssp. canadensis	black elderberry	0.08
Smilax tamnoides	bristly greenbriar	0.07
Solanum dulcamara[1]	climbing nightshade	0.12
Viburnum opulus var. americanum	cranberrybush	0.03
Viburnum rafinesqueanum	downy arrowwood	0.02
Vitis riparia	riverbank grape	1.55
Zanthoxylum americanum	prickly ash	0.32

[1] non-native

Green Ash-Box Elder Forests

The green ash-box elder forest type was dominated primarily by green ash (*Fraxinus pennsylvanica* Marsh.) but with abundant box elder and hackberry (*Celtis occidentalis* L.). Plot ownership and locations include Ft. Snelling State Park/National Cemetery (5140), Minnesota DNR/Ft. Snelling State Park (5052, 5104), Minnesota DNR/land east of Hastings (5021), Minnesota DNR/Gores Pool WMA (5010, 5034, 5042). Geographically, of these seven plots, three were within 2 km of the confluence of the Minnesota and Mississippi Rivers and four were downstream from Hastings. Green ash was the most abundant species comprising 39% of the total individuals, although the basal area of silver maple was greatest at 10.79 m^2/ha (Table 8).

The density-diameter graph of green ash-box elder forests shows increased density of green ash in smaller size classes suggesting this species is successfully regenerating. In contrast, the density of other prominent taxa in this forest type (elm, hackberry, box elder) are generally consistent across the small and mid-size classes (Figure 6).

Table 8. Basal area and tree density in green ash-box elder forests at Mississippi NRRA, 2011.

Latin name	Common name	Basal area (m²/ha)	Density (trees/ha)
Acer negundo	box elder	3.04	75.12
Acer nigrum	black maple	0.01	3.17
Acer saccharinum	silver maple	10.79	43.78
Celtis occidentalis	hackberry	2.78	96.12
Fraxinus pennsylvanica	green ash	9.70	196.21
Morus alba	white mulberry	0.00	1.76
Ulmus sp.	elm	1.54	86.27
Total		27.86	502.43

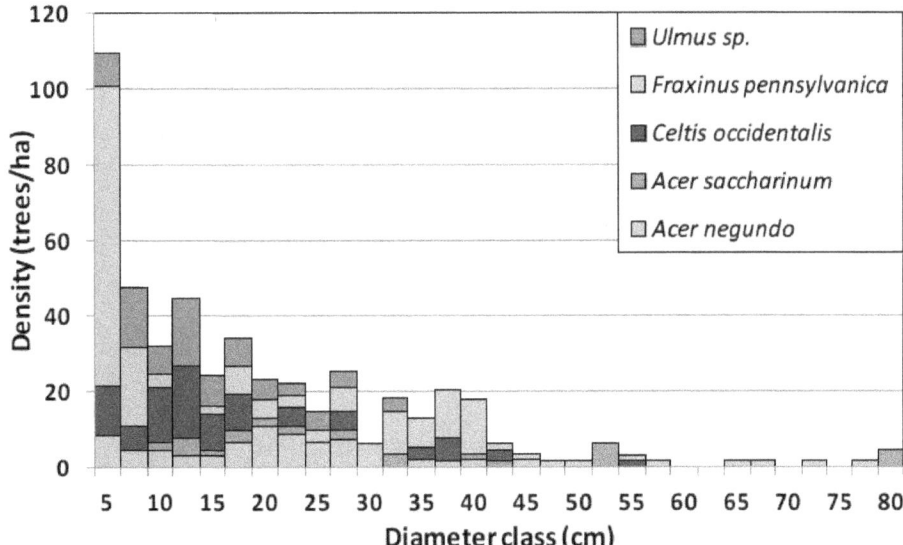

Figure 6. Densities and diameter classes of tree species in green ash-box elder forests at Mississippi NRRA, 2011.

Of the four forest types sampled, seedling density was the lowest in green ash-box elder forests (1,312 seedlings/ha, Table 9). Green ash seedlings represented 47% of the total, with the remaining five species having densities less than 250 seedlings/ha (Table 9).

Table 9. Seedling density in green ash-box elder forests at Mississippi NRRA, 2011.

Latin name	Common name	Density (seedlings/ha)
Acer negundo	box elder	153.44
Acer saccharinum	silver maple	142.86
Celtis occidentalis	hackberry	158.73
Fraxinus pennsylvanica	green ash	619.05
Ulmus sp.	elm	238.10
Total		1,312.17

Fourteen shrub and woody vine species were recorded in green ash-box elder plots with all of these having <1% cover (Table 10). There were three non-native shrub taxa located in these plots.

Table 10. Shrub percent cover in green ash-box elder forests at Mississippi NRRA, 2011.

Latin name	Common name	% Cover
Cornus alternifolia	alternate-leaved dogwood	0.31
Euonymus atropurpurea	burningbush	0.05
Menispermum canadense	moonseed	0.17
Parthenocissus sp.	virginia creeper	0.33
Rhamnus cathartica[1]	buckthorn	0.71
Ribes hirtellum	hairystem gooseberry	0.14
Sambucus nigra ssp. *canadensis*	black elderberry	0.24
Smilax tamnoides	bristly greenbriar	0.23
Solanum dulcamara[1]	climbing nightshade	0.02
Toxicodendron radicans	poison ivy	0.07
Viburnum lantana[1]	wayfaring tree	0.12
Viburnum lentago	nannyberry	0.24
Vitis riparia	riverbank grape	0.48
Zanthoxylum americanum	prickly ash	0.17

[1]non-native

Silver Maple Forests

The silver maple forest type is riparian and characterized by large diameter silver maples. Six plots were classified in this type and plot ownership and locations include Ramsey County Parks/Battle Creek Regional Park (5111), Minnesota DNR/land east of Hastings (5086), and the Minnesota DNR/Gores Pool WMA (5030, 5035, 5106, 5142). Geographically, one of these was adjacent to Pig's Eye Lake and five were within or adjacent to the Gores Pool WMA. Silver maple comprised 76% of the individuals and represented 86% of the basal area (Table 11). Silver maple density decreased in the smallest size classes with only two individuals in the 2.5-5 cm DBH size class (Figure 7). There was a low density of silver maple seedlings detected in the plots (Table 12). Nine shrub and woody vine taxa were recorded in silver maple forests and cover was <1% for all of these (Table 13).

Table 11. Basal area and tree density in silver maple forests at Mississippi NRRA, 2011.

Latin name	Common name	Basal area (m²/ha)	Density (trees/ha)
Acer negundo	box elder	1.27	22.22
Acer saccharinum	silver maple	35.27	237.96
Celtis occidentalis	hackberry	0.02	1.85
Fraxinus nigra	black ash	0.52	3.70
Fraxinus pennsylvanica	green ash	0.03	3.70
Populus deltoides ssp. *monilifera*	cottonwood	3.41	11.11
Ulmus sp.	elm	0.62	29.63
Total		41.14	310.17

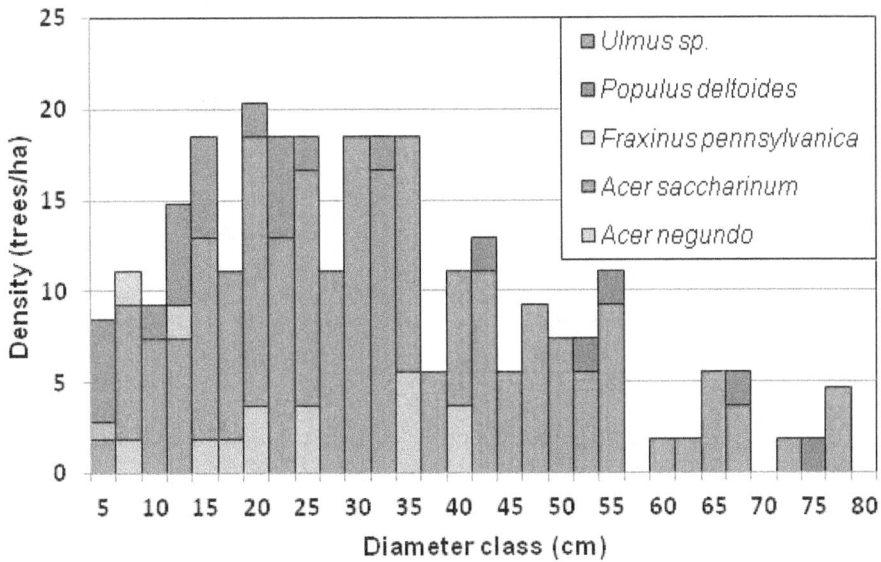

Figure 7. Densities and diameter classes of tree species in silver maple forests at Mississippi NRRA, 2011.

17

Table 12. Seedling density in silver maple forests at Mississippi NRRA, 2011.

Latin name	Common name	Density seedlings/ha
Acer negundo	box elder	555.56
Acer saccharinum	silver maple	55.56
Celtis occidentalis	hackberry	166.67
Fraxinus nigra	black ash	166.67
Fraxinus pennsylvanica	green ash	1,166.67
Ulmus sp.	elm	111.11
Total		2,222.22

Table 13. Shrub percent cover in silver maple forests at Mississippi NRRA, 2011.

Latin name	Common name	% Cover
Menispermum canadense	moonseed	0.17
Parthenocissus sp.	Virginia creeper	0.14
Rhamnus cathartica[1]	buckthorn	0.06
Ribes americanum	American black current	0.03
Ribes cynosbati	eastern prickly gooseberry	0.03
Sambucus nigra ssp. *canadensis*	black elderberry	0.11
Sambucus sp.	elderberry	0.03
Smilax tamnoides	bristly greenbriar	0.28
Solanum dulcamara[1]	climbing nightshade	0.03
Vitis riparia	riverbank grape	0.72

[1] non-native

Coarse Woody Material

Coarse woody material (CWM) varied somewhat between habitats with upland sites having the least volume (36.87 m^3/ha) and biomass (13,509 kg/ha, Table 14). The density of CWM pieces did not vary greatly between habitats (Table 15). The density of standing dead trees of ≥30 DBH ranged from 7.77 – 11.10/ha (Table 16).

Table 14. Coarse woody material volume and biomass for each forest type at Mississippi NRRA, 2011.

Forest type	Number of plots in forest type	Volume (m^3/ha)	Biomass (kg/ha)	Biomass (tons/ac)
Upland	10	36.87	13,509.08	6.03
Cottonwood-box elder	10	68.15	22,919.32	10.22
Green ash-box elder	7	50.33	18,233.19	8.13
Silver maple	6	39.52	14,595.02	6.51
Mean		49.77	17,570.16	7.84

18

Table 15. Coarse woody material density in four diameter classes at Mississippi NRRA, 2011.

| Forest type | Density (pieces/ha) in diameter classes (cm) | | | | Total |
	7.5-19.9	20-32.9	33-45.9	≥46	pieces/ha
Upland	332.86	51.68	3.75	1.56	389.85
Cottonwood-box elder	254.18	33.32	4.30	9.25	301.05
Green ash-box elder	250.80	63.67	19.51	2.76	336.74
Silver maple	357.21	37.80	5.13	5.60	405.75
Mean	296.82	45.67	7.16	4.94	354.59

Table 16. Density of standing dead trees ≥30 cm DBH at Mississippi NRRA, 2011.

Forest type	Density (trees/ha)
Upland	11.10
Cottonwood-box elder	7.77
Green ash-box elder	9.08
Silver maple	11.10

Browse and Disease

Browse pressure at MISS was high in 2011, especially in upland plots, where 55% of browse circles showed evidence of browse (Table 17). In the riparian habitats, 21-36% of browse circles had browsed individuals (Table 17).

Table 17. Direct browse at the 1 m radius browse circles, by forest type and for the whole park.

Forest type	Number of plots	Browse circles with evident browse	Browse circles with species present	Browse index*
Upland	10	367	665	0.5517
Cottonwood-box elder	10	166	461	0.3607
Green ash-box elder	7	49	235	0.2110
Silver maple	6	35	112	0.3158
Whole park	33	617	1,473	0.4190

*The browse index is the ratio of the number of circles with any woody species browsed within the molar zone to the number of circles with any woody species present.

In the indirect browse assessment, we only detected browse on one of the three target herbaceous species, wood nettle, and the extent of browse was low. In upland forests, 5.1% of individuals exhibited browse, while browse extent ranged from 1.3-2.5% of individuals in riparian forests (Table 18).

We did not note the presence of any severe sign of damage or disease. Further, we did not note any D-shaped exit holes on trees which would indicate the presence of emerald ash borer.

le 18. Summary of indirect browse documented at Mississippi NRRA in 2011.

rest type	Species	Number of quadrats where present	Mean maximum height per quadrat	Abundance	Number of unbrowsed and non-reproductive individuals	Number of unbrowsed and reproductive individuals	Nu br ind
and	*Osmorhiza* sp.	8	11.9	13	12	1	
	Maianthemum racemosum	7	20.1	16	15	1	
	Laportea canadensis	21	49.5	156	148	0	
tonwood-box er	*Maianthemum racemosum*	2	29.5	2	2	0	
	Laportea canadensis	159	54.1	3188	3,052	94	
en ash-box er	*Maianthemum racemosum*	2	22	3	3	☐	
	Laportea canadensis	99	47.4	2,219	2,139	25	
er maple	*Laportea canadensis*	73	36.8	1,263	1,166	68	

Community Indices

There were 248 species, collectively, in the 33 plots, with a mean of 42.85 species/plot. Across all forest types, the overwhelming majority were perennial and native (Table 19). Herbaceous species (forb and graminoid) represented 55% of the total and, of those that are pollinated, 65.1% are done so via biotic means.

Table 19. Plot species richness within classes of each functional group.

Functional group	Class	Mean richness 2011
Live history	annual	4.42
	biennial	1.95
	perennial	36.48
Growth form	forb	20.28
	graminoid	3.30
	woody	19.27
Pollination	abiotic	14.33
	biotic	27.91
	N/A	0.61
Nativity	native	35.97
	non-native	6.27
	native/non-native	0.61

Coefficient of conservatism (COC) values ranged from 3.09-3.47 for the four forest types (Figure 8), with a mean for the entire park of 3.35. Mean plot species richness ranged from 20 – 64 across the five forest types (Figure 8).

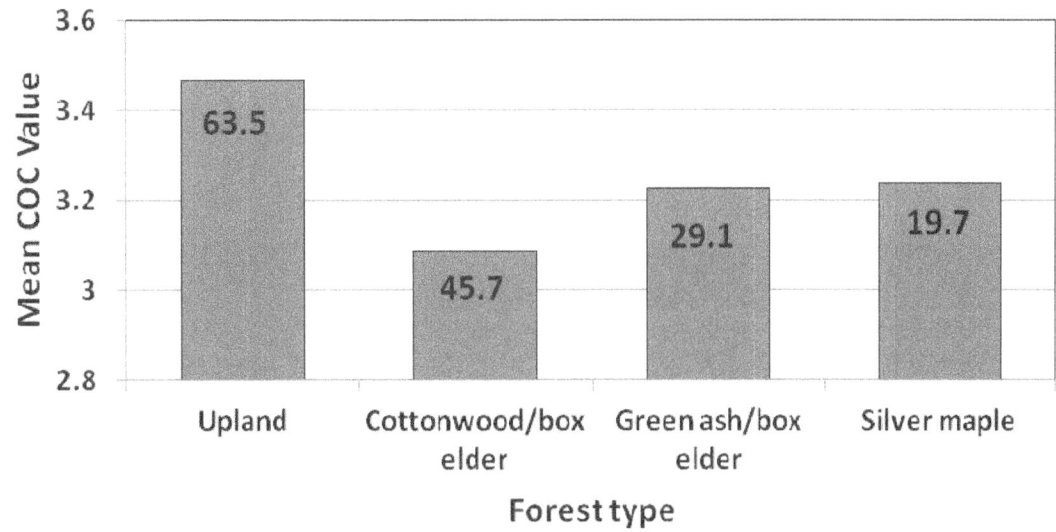

Figure 8. Mean coefficient of conservatism (COC) values for the four forest types. Numbers on the blue bars are the mean plot species richness in those forest types.

Discussion

Ecology and Interpretation

This work demonstrates two serious forest health issues at the Mississippi National River and Recreation Area. Floodplain forests in riparian habitats are diverging from their pre-impoundment species composition and structure, due largely to flow regulation, while upland habitats are impacted by non-native shrub taxa.

In an unimpounded stretch of river, the age structure and spatial distribution of overstory species in floodplains are controlled largely by pulses in stream flow (Hupp 1983, Streng et al. 1989, Nilsson et al. 1991, Johnson 1994, Friedman et al. 1998). Moderate to high flow events scour banks, sandbars, islands, and point bars, creating nursery sites on which seedlings of pioneer species, such as cottonwood and willows, can establish free of competing vegetation. Following germination, these species require a large flow event followed by a gradual decline in flow over the remainder of the initial growing season to survive through that period. In drier climates, such as the North American west, it is critical for survival that the drop in water level is slow enough that root elongation can keep pace; otherwise, dessication of the newly germinated seedlings will occur (Mahoney and Rood 1992). While this is still true in mesic areas, such as the upper Midwest, the availability of summer rainfall can buffer fast drops in water levels, providing some protection against mid- and late-summer dessication (Stewart Rood, University of Lethbridge, personal communication). Establishment can then occur if ice scour is low in the first two springs following germination and flow levels are such that anoxia of growing seedlings does not occur during this time. Because this specific set of conditions occurs only periodically, cohorts of these species develop, with the time between cohorts ranging between approximately 5-10 years (Mahoney and Rood 1998). We did not observe any cottonwood seedling at any site in the 2011 sampling at MISS. Our criteria for recognizing seedlings is that they be at least 15 cm in height and show evidence of previous year's growth. As such, any seedlings identified would be in at least their second growing season. The current year's cottonwood seeds were releasing throughout most of the time we sampled. In addition to not detecting seedlings, we did not observe any of the current year's germinants.

Channelizing the river also hinders regeneration. In a non-channelized river, the streambed meanders over time so that, where the river bends, the outside banks are constantly eroding away while deposition is constantly occurring on the inside banks. This newly created habitat is easily cleared by floods, and is ideal for seedling growth of pioneer floodplain species such as cottonwoods. Levees and other reinforcing structures throughout much of the upper Mississippi River prevent the river from meandering, a natural, healthy process as rivers age.

Dams, as well as levees (Gergel et al. 2002) eliminate the annual pulse-low flow cycle of rivers, moderating heavy flow events and supplementing natural flow during typical low flow periods of mid- to late-summer. They also influence physiographical processes, particularly downstream of the dam. Collectively, these changes can reduce the abundance of disturbance-dependent species, such as cottonwoods and willows, and cause a transition to later successional plant communities (Junk et al. 1989).

Lock and Dams #1, #2, and #3 on the Mississippi River are in Minneapolis/St. Paul, Hastings, and Red Wing, Minnesota and were erected in 1917, 1907, and 1938 respectively. These impoundments have influenced the riparian vegetation in, and downstream of, the Twin Cities metro area. We did not observe any cottonwood trees smaller than 15 cm, although most were greater than 30 cm (Figures 5, 7). Scott et al. (1997) regressed *Populus deltoides* age on diameters at breast height for a population along the Missouri River in central Montana. Numerous environmental factors affect annual ring widths, and ultimately stem diameter, so age-diameter relationships cannot be assumed to be similar between sites. Nonetheless, their results can serve as a general reference of the size-to-age relationship of cottonwoods. They found a 30 cm DBH individual was predicted to be between 50 and 60 years old, while a 70 cm tree was predicted to be roughly 110 years old. This relationship, combined with our results, suggests that it is possible that there has been minimal cottonwood recruitment on the upper Mississippi River since the establishment of the these dams.

In the absence of flooding disturbance, succession is occurring along the MISS floodplains. Later successional floodplain species such as box elder and elm, in addition to colonizing cottonwoods, are not being replaced in the small diameter size classes, while green ash and hackberry density are increasing. Similar results have been observed by others, including Johnson et al. (2012), who resampled plots along the upper Missouri River in 2008. These plots had initially been sampled in 1969 and 1970, and changes over the ensuing 39-year time period were substantial. They observed marked reductions in both American elm and box elder with only slight decreases in green ash composition.

The altered flooding may be affecting the herbaceous layer, in addition to trees. While we observed numerous non-native species in the understories of riparian plots, two species are particularly invasive and pose a threat to forest integrity. In the 23 plots in floodplain forests, garlic mustard (*Alliaria petiolata* [M. Bieb.] Carava and Grande) was present in 10 (43%) and reed canarygrass (*Phalaris arundinaceae* L.) was present in 13 (57%). Within only those plots where they were present, garlic mustard and reed canarygrass were located in 27% and 22% of the quadrats, respectively. Garlic mustard spreads via prolific seed production, with dispersal aided by stream transport. This seed production, along with its allelopathic properties, early spring growth, and tolerance of moderate flooding, allow garlic mustard to outcompete many native species. Reed canarygrass is indeed a grass, and spreads primarily by a dense network of underground rhizomes, but also via a large number of seeds which, like garlic mustard, are carried downstream. Efforts to control these species are ongoing, and vary by level of effort, control method, and ownership. Garlic mustard has been the focus of many efforts, by both volunteers and paid employees, including both hand pulling and herbicide treatments.

The upland community was much more diverse and varied than the riparian communities. Not only were there more tree and shrub species present, the habitats themselves varied greatly. For example, in sites at Coon Rapids Dam Regional Park, the plots were in mesic, mid-successional stands with large amounts of red maple (*Acer rubrum* L.). In contrast, the plot at Grey Cloud Dunes Scientific and Natural Area was open with high light and species adapted to coarse textured soils. The density-diameter graph (Figure 4) for all plots in the habitat indicates increasing density with decreasing diameter, suggesting the common species are regenerating. In addition to trees, the upland plots had high shrub diversity with a total of 27 species observed within that habitat (Table 4). Two shrub taxa, buckthorn and exotic honeysuckles, are highly invasive and were commonly observed in many upland plots. Both taxa were located in nine of the 10 total upland plots. In the plots where they were present, mean buckthorn cover was 14.4% and honeysuckle cover was 6.8%.

Although characteristics between the upland and the riparian forests vary greatly, all MISS forests face the immediate threat of emerald ash borer (*Agrilus planipennis* Fairmaire). This insect was first discovered in the Twin Cities metro area in 2009 and has been documented in both Hennepin and Ramsey Counties. This species feeds on the phloem layer, disrupting the flow of nutrients within the tree. It is lethal to the tree and there are no known effective control measures.

Ash was present in all forest types at MISS, although in silver maple forests, it only comprised a small fraction of the total component. In contrast, in green ash-box elder forests, green ash comprised 39% of the density and 35% of the basal area. The other two forest types had less ash, although still a significant amount. In upland plots, both green and black ash collectively represented 7% of the density and 6% of the basal area. In cottonwood-box elder forests, ash represented 6% and 18% of the density and basal area, respectively.

The loss of ash in all forest types could be devastating, although particularly so in the uplands. Ash death will result in gaps within which opportunistic species, namely buckthorn and honeysuckle, can more easily gain a foothold over native species. It is unclear how the loss of ash will impact riparian forests. The successional trajectories are already disrupted with altered hydrology. Green ash is now occupying the niche vacated by species requiring flooding. The impending loss of green ash will reopen this niche.

Management Directions

Because the upper Mississippi River is managed for navigation, industry, and recreation, large-scale management for forest composition and structure is not likely. Nonetheless, some smaller-scale efforts are being made. A Water Level Management Task Force has been assembled to assess the impacts of, and carry out, pool drawdowns on the upper Mississippi River. To date, all drawdowns have occurred downstream from MISS. Pool 8 was drawn down in 2001 and 2002, Pool 5 in 2005 and 2006, and Pool 6 in 2010. Efforts are underway to initiate a drawdown of Pool 3, which is between Hastings and Red Wing, Minnesota. A large amount of MISS land is within the Pool 3 basin, as are 12 long-term monitoring plots. This land includes the Gores Pool Wildlife Management Area, downstream from Hastings, Minnesota.

This effort may allow a new cohort of cottonwoods to become established. Cottonwoods are a foundation species (Dayton 1972) in pioneer riparian and later successional secondary floodplain habitats. As such, they provide habitat for other species. Steenhof et al. (1980) studied habitat use by overwintering eagles on the Missouri River in southern South Dakota. They found the proportion of cottonwoods among the trees used by eagles was greater than the overall proportion of cottonwoods in the study area. Moreover, box elder, American elm, and green ash were present in greater proportions in the study area than the proportion of trees used by eagles. The continued loss of cottonwoods at MISS could limit eagle nests and require eagles to fly farther for food. The consequences of this altered habitat could result in further stresses on eagles and contribute to reductions in reproductive rates.

Invasive species are a huge issue for park managers in the various units that comprise the park. Continued, or increased, control of garlic mustard, reed canarygrass, buckthorn, and honeysuckle are essential. Nonetheless, there are numerous areas within the riverway with little to no impacts by invasives. Maintaining or improving habitat will promote forest integrity as a whole. This is especially relevent with the impending arrival of the emerald ash borer.

Implementation: Problems, Logistics, and Future Plans

Sampling in 2011 at MISS was somewhat problematic due to the high water levels in June. We had a target to complete at least 45 plots, although only 32 were completed. We postponed sampling all plots in the Gores Pool WMA until the last scheduled work there, and during this time additional flooding occurred. In the future, we would like to sample additional plots in this area. Unfortunately, our sampling schedule does not permit us to spend an entire summer there.

Literature Cited

Bernthal, T. W. 2003. Development of a Floristic Quality Assessment Methodology for Wisconsin. CD975115-01-0, Wisconsin Department of Natural Resources.

Brown, J. K. 1974. Handbook for Inventorying Downed Woody Material. USDA Forest Service General Technical Report INT-16. Intermountain Forest & Range Experiment Station, Ogden, Utah.

Dayton, P. K. 1972. Toward an understanding of community resilience and the potential effects of enrichments to the benthos at McMurdo Sound, Antarctica. *in* B. C. Parker, editor. Proceedings of the colloquium on conservation problems in Antarctica. Lawrence, KS: Allen Press.

Dyer, J. M. 2006. Revisiting the deciduous forests of eastern North America. BioScience 56:341-352.

Elliott, K. J., and W. T. Swank. 2008. Long-term changes in forest composition and diversity following early logging (1919-1923) and the decline of American chestnut (*Castanea dentata*). Plant Ecology 197:155-172.

Friedman, J. M., W. R. Osterkamp, M. L. Scott, and G. T. Auble. 1998. Downstream effects of dams on channel geometry and bottomland vegetation: regional patterns in the Great Plains. Wetlands 18:619-633.

Gergel, S. E., M. D. Dixon, and M. G. Turner. 2002. Consequences of human-altered floods: levees, floods, and floodplain forests along the Wisconsin River. Ecological Applications 12:1755-1770.

Hupp, C. R. 1983. Vegetation pattern on channel features in the Passage Creek Gorge, Virginia. Castanea 48:62-72.

Johnson, S. E., E. L. Mudrak, E. A. Beever, S. Sanders, and D. M. Waller. 2008. Comparing power among three sampling methods for monitoring forest vegetation. Canadian Journal of Forest Research 38:143-156.

Johnson, S. E., E. L. Mudrak, and D. M. Waller. 2006. A comparison of sampling methodologies for long-term monitoring of forest vegetation in the Great Lakes Network National Parks. National Park Service, Great Lakes Network Office, Ashland, Wisconsin.

Johnson, W. C. 1994. Woodland expansion in the Platte River, Nebraska: patterns and causes. Ecological Monographs 64:45-84.

Johnson, W. C., M. D. Dixon, M. L. Scott, L. Rabbe, G. Larson, M. Volke, and B. Werner. 2012. Forty years of vegetation change on the Missouri River floodplain. BioScience 62:123-135.

Junk, W., J., P. B. Bayley, and R. E. Sparks. 1989. The flood pulse concept in river-floodplain systems. Pages 110-127 in D. P. Dodge, editor. Proceedings of the International Large River Symposium. Canadian Special Publication Fisheries Aquatic Sciences.

Leete, P., and B. Richardson. 1999. Minnesota Land Cover Classification System. Minnesota Department of Natural Resources, St. Paul.

Mahoney, J. M., and S. B. Rood. 1992. Response of a hybrid poplar to water table decline in different substrates. Forest Ecology and Management 54:141-156.

Mahoney, J. M., and S. B. Rood. 1998. Streamflow requirements for cottonwood seedling recruitment-an integrative model. Wetlands 18:634-345.

Milburn, S. A., M. Bourdaghs, and J. J. Husveth. 2007. Floristic Quality Assessment for Minnesota Wetlands. Minnesota Pollution Control Agency, St. Paul, Minnesota.

Morellet, N., P. Ballon, Y. Boscardin, and S. Champely. 2003. A new index to measure roe deer (*Capreolus capreolus*) browsing pressure on woody flora. Game and Wildlife Science 20:155-173.

Morellet, N., S. Champely, J.-M. Gaillard, P. Ballon, and Y. Boscardin. 2001. The browsing index: new tool uses browsing pressure to monitor deer populations. Wildlife Society Bulletin 29:1243-1252.

Nilsson, C., A. Ekblad, M. Gardfjell, and B. Carlberg. 1991. Long-term effects of river regulation on river margin vegetation. Journal of Applied Ecology 28:963-987.

Scott, M. L., G. T. Auble, and J. M. Friedman. 1997. Flood dependency of cottonwood establishment along the Missouri River, Montana, USA. Ecological Applications 7:677-690.

Smith, W. R. 2008. Trees and Shrubs of Minnesota. University of Minnesota Press, Minneapolis.

Steenhof, K., S. S. Berlinger, and L. H. Fredrickson. 1980. Habitat use by wintering bald eagles in South Dakota. Journal of Wildlife Management 44:798-805.

Streng, D. R., J. S. Glitzenstein, and P. A. Harcombe. 1989. Woody seedling dynamics in an east Texas floodplain forest. Ecological Monographs 59:177-204.

Stevens, D. L., and A. R. Olsen. 2004. Spatially balanced sampling of natural resources. Journal of the American Statistical Association 99:262-278.

U.S. Department of Agriculture. 2010. IPED Field Guide Pest Evaluation and Detection. Northeastern Areas State and Private Forestry. Newtown Square, PA.

U.S. Department of Agriculture. 2005. Forest Inventory and Analysis National Core Field Guide. U.S. Department of Agriculture, Forest Service, Arlington, Virginia.

Woodall, C. W., and V. J. Monleon. 2007. Sampling Protocol, Estimation, and Analysis Procedures for the Down Woody Materials Indicator of the FIA program., U.S. Forest Service, Newtown Square.

Appendix A. Field Site Maps

Note: The field site maps are not included in electronic versions of this report in order to minimize file size. If you would like copies of these, either electronically or in print, please contact the Great Lakes Inventory and Monitoring Network office.

Appendix B. Complete List of Species Sampled

Species Encountered during Site Visits - by Park

Park: MISS   Year: 2011

This information is from certified and uncertified data from standard sampling of active alternating plots at this park.

Species

HERBACEOUS - Fern / Fern Allies

Dryopteridaceae
Athyrium filix-femina ssp. angustum
Cystopteris fragilis
Matteuccia struthiopteris
Onoclea sensibilis

Equisetaceae
Equisetum arvense
Equisetum hyemale
Equisetum pratense

Ophioglossaceae
Botrychium sp.
Botrychium virginianum

Osmundaceae
Osmunda cinnamomea

Pteridaceae
Adiantum pedatum

HERBACEOUS - Forb

Alismataceae
Sagittaria latifolia

Amaranthaceae
Amaranthus retroflexus
Chenopodium album
Chenopodium simplex

Apiaceae
Angelica atropurpurea
Cicuta maculata
Cryptotaenia canadensis
Daucus carota
Heracleum sphondylium ssp. montanum
Osmorhiza claytonii
Osmorhiza sp.
Sanicula marilandica
Sanicula odorata
Sanicula sp.

Araceae
Arisaema dracontium
Arisaema triphyllum
Lemna minor

Araliaceae
Hydrocotyle americana

Aristolochiaceae
Asarum canadense

Asparagaceae
Polygonatum biflorum
Polygonatum pubescens

Asparagaceae
Maianthemum canadense
Maianthemum racemosum

Asparagaceae
Maianthemum stellatum

Asteraceae
Ambrosia trifida
Arctium minus
Asteraceae fam.
Bidens cernua
Bidens connata
Bidens frondosa
Bidens sp.
Cirsium altissimum
Cirsium arvense
Cirsium discolor
Cirsium sp.
Erigeron annuus
Erigeron philadelphicus
Erigeron sp.
Eurybia macrophylla
Lactuca canadensis
Prenanthes a ba
Rudbeckia laciniata
Solidago flexicaulis
Solidago sp.
Taraxacum officinale

Balsaminaceae
Impatiens capensis
Impatiens sp.

Berberidaceae
Caulophyllum thalictroides

Boraginaceae
Hackelia virginiana
Hydrophyllum virginianum

Brassicaceae
Alliaria petiolata
Cardamine impatiens
Cardamine pensylvanica
Hesperis matronalis

Cannabaceae
Cannabis sativa

Caprifoliaceae
Triosteum perfoliatum

Caryophyllaceae
Cerastium fontanum ssp. vulgare
Cerastium sp.
Moehringia lateriflora
Myosoton aquaticum
Stellaria media

Ceratophyllaceae
Ceratophyllum demersum

Colchicaceae
Uvularia grandiflora
Uvularia sessilifolia

Euphorbiaceae
Acalypha rhomboidea

Fabaceae
Desmodium canadense
Desmodium glutinosum
Desmodium sp.
Medicago lupulina
Trifolium pratense
Trifolium repens

Geraniaceae
Geranium maculatum

Iridaceae
Iris pseudacorus
Iris versicolor

Lamiaceae
Glechoma hederacea
Lamiaceae fam.
Leonurus cardiaca
Lycopus americanus
Lycopus sp.
Lycopus uniflorus
Nepeta cataria
Scutellaria sp.
Stachys palustris
Stachys sp.
Stachys tenuifolia
Teucrium canadense

Liliaceae
Streptopus lanceolatus var. roseus

Melanthiaceae
Trillium sp.

Onagraceae
Circaea lutetiana ssp. canadensis

Orchidaceae
Galearis spectabilis
Orchidaceae fam.

Oxalidaceae
Oxalis sp.
Oxalis stricta

Papaveraceae
Chelidonium majus
Sanguinaria canadensis

Plantaginaceae
Plantago major
Plantago rugelii

Plantaginaceae
Veronica sp.

Polemoniaceae
Phlox divaricata

Polygonaceae
Fallopia convolvulus
Persicaria virginiana
Rumex crispus
Rumex obtusifolius
Rumex sp.

Primulaceae
Lysimachia ciliata

Primulaceae
Lysimachia nummularia

Pyrolaceae
Pyrola elliptica
Pyrola sp.

Ranunculaceae
Actaea rubra
Actaea sp.
Anemone canadensis
Anemone quinquefolia
Anemone virginiana
Aquilegia canadensis
Caltha palustris
Clematis virginiana
Ranunculus abortivus
Ranunculus fascicularis
Ranunculus hispidus
Ranunculus sceleratus
Ranunculus sp.
Thalictrum dasycarpum
Thalictrum dioicum
Thalictrum thalictroides

Rosaceae
Agrimonia striata
Fragaria vesca
Fragaria virginiana
Geum aleppicum
Geum laciniatum
Geum sp.
Potentilla anserina ssp. anserina
Potentilla simplex

Rubiaceae
Galium aparine
Galium asprellum
Galium boreale
Galium sp.
Galium trifidum
Galium triflorum

Scrophulariaceae
Scrophularia lanceolata
Verbascum thapsus

Solanaceae
Solanum ptychanthum

Typhaceae
Sparganium sp.

Urticaceae
Boehmeria cylindrica
Laportea canadensis
Pilea pumila
Pilea sp.
Urtica dioica ssp. gracilis

Violaceae
Viola pubescens
Viola sp.

Xanthorrhoeaceae
Hemerocallis fulva

HERBACEOUS - Forb (vine)

Convolvulaceae
  Calystegia sepium

Cucurbitaceae
  Cucurbitaceae fam.
  Echinocystis lobata
  Sicyos angulatus

Dioscoreaceae
  Dioscorea villosa

Fabaceae
  Amphicarpaea bracteata

Smilacaceae
  Smilax ecirrata
  Smilax sp.

HERBACEOUS - Graminoid

Cyperaceae
  Carex assiniboinensis
  Carex bebbii
  Carex blanda
  Carex deweyana
  Carex gracillima
  Carex grisea
  Carex pedunculata
  Carex pensylvanica
  Carex projecta
  Carex radiata
  Carex rosea
  Carex sp.
  Carex sprengelii
  Carex stipata
  Scirpus sp.

Poaceae
  Brachyelytrum erectum
  Bromus inermis
  Calamagrostis canadensis
  Cinna arundinacea
  Elymus sp.
  Elymus virginicus
  Leersia oryzoides
  Phalaris arundinacea
  Poa compressa
  Poa pratensis
  Poa sp.
  Poaceae fam.

SHRUB

Adoxaceae
  Sambucus nigra ssp. canadensis
  Sambucus racemosa var. racemosa
  Sambucus sp.
  Viburnum lantana
  Viburnum lentago
  Viburnum opulus var. americanum
  Viburnum rafinesqueanum
  Viburnum sp.

Berberidaceae
  Berberis thunbergii
  Berberis vulgaris

Betulaceae
  Corylus americana

Caprifoliaceae
  Lonicera (exotic) sp.
  Lonicera morrowii
  Lonicera sp.
  Lonicera xylosteum
  Symphoricarpos occidentalis

Celastraceae
  Euonymus atropurpurea

Cornaceae
  Cornus alternifolia
  Cornus amomum
  Cornus racemosa
  Cornus sericea
  Cornus sp.

Grossulariaceae
  Ribes americanum
  Ribes cynosbati
  Ribes hirtellum
  Ribes sp.

Rhamnaceae
  Rhamnus cathartica
  Rhamnus frangula

Rosaceae
  Amelanchier Group 2 sp.
  Amelanchier Group 3 sp.
  Physocarpus opulifolius
  Rosa carolina
  Rubus idaeus ssp. strigosus
  Rubus occidentalis
  Rubus pensilvanicus
  Rubus pubescens
  Rubus semisetosus
  Rubus setosus

Rutaceae
  Zanthoxylum americanum

Salicaceae
  Salix sp.

Sapindaceae
  Acer ginnala

Staphyleaceae
  Staphylea trifolia

SHRUB - Woody Vine

Anacardiaceae
  Toxicodendron radicans
  Toxicodendron rydbergii

Cannabaceae
  Humulus lupulus

Menispermaceae
  Menispermum canadense

Smilacaceae
  Smilax tamnoides

Solanaceae
  Solanum dulcamara

Vitaceae
  Parthenocissus quinquefolia
  Parthenocissus sp.
  Vitis riparia

TREE

Betulaceae
  Betula nigra
  Betula papyrifera
  Betula sp.
  Ostrya virginiana

Cupressaceae
  Juniperus virginiana

Fabaceae
  Gleditsia triacanthos
  Gymnocladus dioicus

Fagaceae
  Quercus alba
  Quercus ellipsoidalis
  Quercus macrocarpa
  Quercus rubra
  Quercus sp.

Juglandaceae
  Carya cordiformis
  Juglans cinerea
  Juglans nigra
  Juglans sp.

Malvaceae
  Tilia americana

Moraceae
  Morus alba
  Morus rubra

Oleaceae
  Fraxinus nigra
  Fraxinus pennsylvanica
  Fraxinus sp.

Pinaceae
  Abies balsamea

Rosaceae
  Crataegus sp.
  Prunus pensylvanica
  Prunus serotina
  Prunus sp.
  Prunus virginiana

Salicaceae
  Populus deltoides ssp. monilifera
  Populus grandidentata
  Populus tremuloides
  Salix amygdaloides
  Salix nigra

Sapindaceae
  Acer negundo
  Acer nigrum
  Acer rubrum
  Acer saccharinum
  Acer saccharum
  Aesculus glabra

Ulmaceae
  Celtis occidentalis
  Ulmus americana
  Ulmus pumila
  Ulmus rubra
  Ulmus sp.

Appendix C. Individual Plot Data

Density and Basal Area of Tree Species (Live trees)

Plot: 5002

Species	Density (individuals / ha)	Basal Area (m²/ ha)
hardwood		
Acer negundo	77.8	0.7
Betula papyrifera	11.1	1.0
Carya cordiformis	388.9	6.4
Celtis occidentalis	511.1	2.0
Fraxinus pennsylvanica	66.7	4.9
Ostrya virginiana	33.3	0.4
Prunus serotina	66.7	5.4
Prunus virginiana	11.1	0.0
Quercus rubra	11.1	1.8
Tilia americana	22.2	0.0
Ulmus americana	11.1	0.0
Ulmus rubra	44.4	1.0
TOTAL	**1,255.6**	**23.8**

Plot: 5004

Species	Density (individuals / ha)	Basal Area (m²/ ha)
hardwood		
Acer negundo	177.8	6.0
Acer saccharinum	88.9	4.1
Fraxinus pennsylvanica	33.3	1.3
Gleditsia triacanthos	11.1	0.3
Populus deltoides ssp. monilifera	55.6	3.1
Ulmus rubra	233.3	1.2
TOTAL	**600.0**	**16.0**

Plot: 5006

Species	Density (individuals / ha)	Basal Area (m²/ ha)
hardwood		
Acer nigrum	11.1	0.0
Carya cordiformis	188.9	2.4
Celtis occidentalis	77.8	0.9
Fraxinus nigra	33.3	0.1
Fraxinus pennsylvanica	88.9	0.8
Ostrya virginiana	111.1	0.5
Prunus serotina	22.2	0.1
Quercus macrocarpa	11.1	0.0
Tilia americana	66.7	0.4
Ulmus americana	33.3	0.2
Ulmus rubra	77.8	0.6
softwood		
Juniperus virginiana	155.6	1.4
TOTAL	**877.8**	**7.4**

Plot: 5010

Species	Density (individuals / ha)	Basal Area (m²/ ha)
hardwood		
Acer negundo	11.1	0.0
Acer saccharinum	22.2	26.4
Fraxinus pennsylvanica	77.8	20.1
Ulmus rubra	33.3	0.6
TOTAL	**144.4**	**47.0**

Plot: 5016

Species	Density (individuals / ha)	Basal Area (m²/ ha)
hardwood		
Acer negundo	222.2	5.7
Acer saccharinum	148.1	6.8
Celtis occidentalis	37.0	1.2
Fraxinus pennsylvanica	98.8	4.4
Juglans nigra	49.4	0.2
Morus alba	12.3	0.3
Populus deltoides ssp. monilifera	37.0	14.3
Ulmus rubra	24.7	0.4
TOTAL	**629.6**	**33.5**

Plot: 5018

Species	Density (individuals / ha)	Basal Area (m²/ ha)
hardwood		
Betula papyrifera	266.7	5.2
Carya cordiformis	77.8	0.1
Celtis occidentalis	11.1	0.0
Fraxinus pennsylvanica	100.0	1.7
Ostrya virginiana	33.3	0.2
Populus deltoides ssp. monilifera	44.4	5.0
Prunus serotina	11.1	0.0
Prunus virginiana	11.1	0.0
Quercus macrocarpa	11.1	0.1
Quercus rubra	233.3	2.4
Tilia americana	411.1	1.6
Ulmus americana	155.6	0.4
Ulmus rubra	200.0	1.4
TOTAL	**1,566.7**	**18.0**

Plot: 5020

Species	Density (individuals / ha)	Basal Area (m²/ ha)
hardwood		
Acer negundo	122.2	4.2
Acer saccharinum	133.3	7.9
Celtis occidentalis	11.1	0.1
Fraxinus nigra	211.1	1.5
Fraxinus pennsylvanica	155.6	2.9
Populus deltoides ssp. monilifera	55.6	8.3
Prunus virginiana	11.1	0.0
Salix nigra	11.1	2.3
TOTAL	**711.1**	**27.3**

Plot: 5021	Density (individuals / ha)	Basal Area (m²/ ha)
Species		
hardwood		
Acer negundo	22.2	0.6
Acer saccharinum	55.6	0.8
Fraxinus pennsylvanica	288.9	25.4
Ulmus rubra	144.4	3.0
TOTAL	**511.1**	**29.9**

Plot: 5022	Density (individuals / ha)	Basal Area (m²/ ha)
Species		
hardwood		
Acer negundo	111.1	2.8
Acer saccharinum	211.1	24.4
Fraxinus pennsylvanica	44.4	1.0
Populus deltoides ssp. monilifera	88.9	20.3
Ulmus rubra	33.3	0.7
TOTAL	**488.9**	**49.2**

Plot: 5030	Density (individuals / ha)	Basal Area (m²/ ha)
Species		
hardwood		
Acer saccharinum	16.7	7.4
TOTAL	**16.7**	**7.4**

Plot: 5031	Density (individuals / ha)	Basal Area (m²/ ha)
Species		
hardwood		
Acer negundo	155.6	3.6
Betula papyrifera	22.2	1.2
Populus deltoides ssp. monilifera	33.3	7.3
Prunus serotina	22.2	0.7
Prunus virginiana	11.1	0.0
Quercus macrocarpa	11.1	0.1
Quercus rubra	144.4	5.5
Ulmus rubra	88.9	2.5
TOTAL	**488.9**	**20.8**

Plot: 5033	Density (individuals / ha)	Basal Area (m²/ ha)
Species		
hardwood		
Acer negundo	11.1	0.2
Celtis occidentalis	44.4	1.5
Prunus serotina	11.1	0.5
Quercus macrocarpa	144.4	15.0
Tilia americana	33.3	2.2
Ulmus rubra	244.4	3.4
TOTAL	**488.9**	**22.8**

Plot: 5034	Density (individuals / ha)	Basal Area (m²/ ha)
Species		
hardwood		
Acer negundo	87.0	6.7
Acer saccharinum	43.5	1.6
Ulmus rubra	101.4	3.2
TOTAL	**231.9**	**11.5**

Plot: 5035	Density (individuals / ha)	Basal Area (m²/ ha)
Species		
hardwood		
Acer negundo	44.4	2.5
Acer saccharinum	211.1	53.2
Celtis occidentalis	11.1	0.1
Fraxinus nigra	22.2	3.1
Ulmus rubra	55.6	2.2
TOTAL	**344.4**	**61.2**

Plot: 5038	Density (individuals / ha)	Basal Area (m²/ ha)
Species		
hardwood		
Acer saccharinum	177.8	19.0
Celtis occidentalis	11.1	0.3
Fraxinus pennsylvanica	44.4	0.9
Juglans cinerea	11.1	3.3
Populus deltoides ssp. monilifera	11.1	28.8
Ulmus rubra	88.9	1.7
TOTAL	**344.4**	**53.9**

Plot: 5039	Density (individuals / ha)	Basal Area (m²/ ha)
Species		
hardwood		
Acer negundo	11.1	0.0
Fraxinus nigra	155.6	0.5
Fraxinus pennsylvanica	33.3	0.1
Populus tremuloides	22.2	1.7
Prunus serotina	133.3	0.7
Quercus alba	66.7	12.4
Quercus macrocarpa	44.4	6.5
Quercus rubra	33.3	0.5
Tilia americana	111.1	0.8
Ulmus rubra	300.0	2.0
TOTAL	**911.1**	**25.3**

Plot: 5042	Density (individuals / ha)	Basal Area (m²/ ha)
Species		
hardwood		
Acer negundo	33.3	0.8
Acer saccharinum	33.3	7.1
Celtis occidentalis	466.7	10.4
Fraxinus pennsylvanica	200.0	18.1
Ulmus rubra	33.3	1.5
TOTAL	**766.7**	**37.8**

Plot: 5052	Density (individuals / ha)	Basal Area (m²/ ha)
Species		
hardwood		
Acer negundo	16.7	0.9
Acer saccharinum	66.7	17.7
Fraxinus pennsylvanica	250.0	0.7
Ulmus rubra	200.0	2.0
TOTAL	533.3	21.3

Plot: 5056	Density (individuals / ha)	Basal Area (m²/ ha)
Species		
hardwood		
Acer negundo	222.2	3.7
Acer saccharinum	55.6	10.1
Celtis occidentalis	88.9	1.5
Fraxinus pennsylvanica	233.3	4.0
Populus deltoides ssp. monilifera	44.4	35.3
Ulmus rubra	233.3	1.5
TOTAL	877.8	56.0

Plot: 5073	Density (individuals / ha)	Basal Area (m²/ ha)
Species		
hardwood		
Carya cordiformis	755.6	14.8
Gymnocladus dioicus	33.3	0.3
Prunus serotina	22.2	0.4
Prunus virginiana	11.1	0.1
Quercus macrocarpa	22.2	6.0
Quercus rubra	11.1	0.2
Ulmus rubra	133.3	4.1
TOTAL	988.9	26.0

Plot: 5076	Density (individuals / ha)	Basal Area (m²/ ha)
Species		
hardwood		
Acer negundo	122.2	1.8
Acer saccharinum	177.8	6.5
Celtis occidentalis	222.2	0.8
Fraxinus pennsylvanica	33.3	0.5
Juglans cinerea	11.1	0.0
Populus deltoides ssp. monilifera	77.8	18.0
Ulmus rubra	33.3	0.1
TOTAL	677.8	27.7

Plot: 5082	Density (individuals / ha)	Basal Area (m²/ ha)
Species		
hardwood		
Carya cordiformis	33.3	0.3
Celtis occidentalis	88.9	0.6
Crataegus sp.	11.1	0.0
Fraxinus pennsylvanica	55.6	3.2
Juglans cinerea	11.1	0.3
Prunus serotina	33.3	0.6
Prunus virginiana	22.2	0.0
Quercus macrocarpa	88.9	7.2
Quercus rubra	33.3	4.1
Tilia americana	444.4	8.1
Ulmus rubra	55.6	0.3
TOTAL	877.8	24.7

Plot: 5084	Density (individuals / ha)	Basal Area (m²/ ha)
Species		
hardwood		
Acer negundo	311.1	4.9
Acer saccharinum	211.1	3.3
Fraxinus pennsylvanica	66.7	1.3
Populus deltoides ssp. monilifera	111.1	9.6
Salix amygdaloides	11.1	2.8
Ulmus rubra	22.2	1.1
TOTAL	733.3	23.1

Plot: 5086	Density (individuals / ha)	Basal Area (m²/ ha)
Species		
hardwood		
Acer negundo	55.6	3.1
Acer saccharinum	355.6	36.8
Populus deltoides ssp. monilifera	55.6	14.6
Ulmus americana	55.6	0.9
Ulmus rubra	11.1	0.3
TOTAL	533.3	55.6

Plot: 5096	Density (individuals / ha)	Basal Area (m²/ ha)
Species		
hardwood		
Acer negundo	111.1	2.7
Celtis occidentalis	11.1	0.2
Prunus serotina	55.6	1.4
Quercus ellipsoidalis	55.6	12.4
Quercus macrocarpa	144.4	21.1
Ulmus rubra	55.6	2.8
TOTAL	433.3	40.7

Plot: 5097

Species	Density (individuals / ha)	Basal Area (m²/ ha)
hardwood		
Acer negundo	22.2	0.1
Acer saccharum	66.7	0.8
Carya cordiformis	33.3	0.1
Celtis occidentalis	300.0	5.1
Fraxinus pennsylvanica	66.7	1.4
Prunus serotina	44.4	2.9
Prunus virginiana	22.2	0.0
Quercus rubra	11.1	3.0
Tilia americana	111.1	4.1
Ulmus rubra	300.0	3.4
TOTAL	**977.8**	**20.8**

Plot: 5099

Species	Density (individuals / ha)	Basal Area (m²/ ha)
hardwood		
Acer negundo	77.8	6.4
Acer saccharinum	77.8	7.5
Betula nigra	11.1	2.2
Celtis occidentalis	11.1	0.9
Populus deltoides ssp. monilifera	22.2	7.3
Ulmus rubra	111.1	3.1
TOTAL	**311.1**	**27.3**

Plot: 5104

Species	Density (individuals / ha)	Basal Area (m²/ ha)
hardwood		
Acer negundo	111.1	2.2
Acer saccharinum	74.1	21.8
Celtis occidentalis	61.7	0.1
Fraxinus pennsylvanica	456.8	2.4
Morus alba	12.3	0.0
Ulmus rubra	24.7	0.1
TOTAL	**740.7**	**26.6**

Plot: 5106

Species	Density (individuals / ha)	Basal Area (m²/ ha)
hardwood		
Acer saccharinum	188.9	20.2
Fraxinus pennsylvanica	22.2	0.2
Populus deltoides ssp. monilifera	11.1	5.9
Ulmus rubra	22.2	0.3
TOTAL	**244.4**	**26.5**

Plot: 5111

Species	Density (individuals / ha)	Basal Area (m²/ ha)
hardwood		
Acer negundo	33.3	2.0
Acer saccharinum	477.8	44.4
TOTAL	**511.1**	**46.5**

Plot: 5140

Species	Density (individuals / ha)	Basal Area (m²/ ha)
hardwood		
Acer negundo	244.4	9.9
Acer nigrum	22.2	0.0
Acer saccharinum	11.1	0.1
Celtis occidentalis	144.4	9.0
Fraxinus pennsylvanica	100.0	1.3
Ulmus rubra	66.7	0.4
TOTAL	**588.9**	**20.8**

Plot: 5142

Species	Density (individuals / ha)	Basal Area (m²/ ha)
hardwood		
Acer saccharinum	177.8	49.6
Ulmus rubra	33.3	0.0
TOTAL	**211.1**	**49.6**

Plot: 5148

Species	Density (individuals / ha)	Basal Area (m²/ ha)
hardwood		
Acer negundo	133.3	6.6
Acer saccharinum	55.6	6.5
Celtis occidentalis	11.1	0.0
Fraxinus pennsylvanica	88.9	2.0
Populus deltoides ssp. monilifera	11.1	6.2
Ulmus rubra	88.9	1.1
TOTAL	**388.9**	**22.3**

Density and Basal Area of Tree Species (Dead trees)

Plot: 5002

Species	Density (individuals / ha)	Basal Area (m²/ ha)
hardwood		
Celtis occidentalis	22.2	0.1
Prunus serotina	11.1	0.5
unknown tree - hardwood	33.3	0.0
softwood / hardwood		
unknown tree	55.6	1.6
TOTAL	**122.2**	**2.2**

Plot: 5004

Species	Density (individuals / ha)	Basal Area (m²/ ha)
hardwood		
Populus deltoides ssp. monilifera	11.1	0.5
unknown tree - hardwood	55.6	0.9
TOTAL	**66.7**	**1.4**

Plot: 5006

Species	Density (individuals / ha)	Basal Area (m²/ ha)
hardwood		
Fraxinus nigra	11.1	0.0
unknown tree - hardwood	44.4	1.0
softwood		
Juniperus virginiana	44.4	0.3
softwood / hardwood		
unknown tree	11.1	0.2
TOTAL	**111.1**	**1.5**

Plot: 5010

Species	Density (individuals / ha)	Basal Area (m²/ ha)
hardwood		
unknown tree - hardwood	22.2	2.3
TOTAL	**22.2**	**2.3**

Plot: 5016

Species	Density (individuals / ha)	Basal Area (m²/ ha)
hardwood		
Acer negundo	24.7	0.1
TOTAL	**24.7**	**0.1**

Plot: 5018

Species	Density (individuals / ha)	Basal Area (m²/ ha)
hardwood		
Betula papyrifera	22.2	0.4
Fraxinus pennsylvanica	11.1	0.0
Populus deltoides ssp. monilifera	22.2	2.6
Tilia americana	33.3	0.1
Ulmus americana	11.1	0.0
Ulmus rubra	11.1	0.0
unknown tree - hardwood	33.3	0.1
TOTAL	**144.4**	**3.2**

Plot: 5020

Species	Density (individuals / ha)	Basal Area (m²/ ha)
hardwood		
Fraxinus nigra	11.1	0.0
unknown tree - hardwood	22.2	0.4
TOTAL	**33.3**	**0.4**

Plot: 5021

Species	Density (individuals / ha)	Basal Area (m²/ ha)
hardwood		
Ulmus rubra	11.1	0.3
unknown tree - hardwood	55.6	1.2
TOTAL	**66.7**	**1.5**

Plot: 5022

Species	Density (individuals / ha)	Basal Area (m²/ ha)
hardwood		
unknown tree - hardwood	11.1	0.3
TOTAL	**11.1**	**0.3**

Plot: 5031

Species	Density (individuals / ha)	Basal Area (m²/ ha)
hardwood		
Acer negundo	11.1	0.1
Betula papyrifera	44.4	2.0
Populus deltoides ssp. monilifera	11.1	0.7
Prunus serotina	11.1	0.1
Quercus rubra	144.4	6.8
Ulmus rubra	11.1	0.2
unknown tree - hardwood	77.8	0.4
TOTAL	**311.1**	**10.1**

Plot: 5033

Species	Density (individuals / ha)	Basal Area (m²/ ha)
hardwood		
Quercus macrocarpa	22.2	0.9
Ulmus rubra	66.7	0.7
unknown tree - hardwood	188.9	3.6
TOTAL	**277.8**	**5.2**

Plot: 5034

Species	Density (individuals / ha)	Basal Area (m²/ ha)
hardwood		
Acer negundo	14.5	1.8
Acer saccharinum	14.5	0.7
Ulmus rubra	29.0	0.8
unknown tree - hardwood	58.0	3.0
TOTAL	**115.9**	**6.3**

Plot: 5035

Species	Density (individuals / ha)	Basal Area (m²/ ha)
hardwood		
Ulmus rubra	11.1	0.0
unknown tree - hardwood	144.4	10.7
TOTAL	155.6	10.7

Plot: 5038

Species	Density (individuals / ha)	Basal Area (m²/ ha)
hardwood		
Acer saccharinum	11.1	0.3
Populus deltoides ssp. monilifera	11.1	1.8
Ulmus rubra	11.1	0.0
unknown tree - hardwood	11.1	1.1
TOTAL	44.4	3.2

Plot: 5039

Species	Density (individuals / ha)	Basal Area (m²/ ha)
hardwood		
Prunus serotina	11.1	0.0
Ulmus rubra	22.2	0.7
unknown tree - hardwood	22.2	0.4
TOTAL	55.6	1.0

Plot: 5052

Species	Density (individuals / ha)	Basal Area (m²/ ha)
hardwood		
unknown tree - hardwood	33.3	0.1
TOTAL	33.3	0.1

Plot: 5056

Species	Density (individuals / ha)	Basal Area (m²/ ha)
hardwood		
Celtis occidentalis	11.1	0.0
Populus deltoides ssp. monilifera	11.1	0.4
unknown tree - hardwood	66.7	0.8
TOTAL	88.9	1.2

Plot: 5073

Species	Density (individuals / ha)	Basal Area (m²/ ha)
hardwood		
Carya cordiformis	66.7	0.4
Celtis occidentalis	11.1	0.0
Ulmus rubra	11.1	0.0
unknown tree - hardwood	44.4	3.4
TOTAL	133.3	3.8

Plot: 5076

Species	Density (individuals / ha)	Basal Area (m²/ ha)
hardwood		
Acer saccharinum	22.2	1.0
unknown tree - hardwood	55.6	0.8
TOTAL	77.8	1.8

Plot: 5082

Species	Density (individuals / ha)	Basal Area (m²/ ha)
hardwood		
Prunus serotina	11.1	0.3
Quercus macrocarpa	33.3	2.5
Tilia americana	11.1	0.1
unknown tree - hardwood	11.1	0.6
TOTAL	66.7	3.5

Plot: 5084

Species	Density (individuals / ha)	Basal Area (m²/ ha)
hardwood		
Acer negundo	77.8	0.3
Acer saccharinum	44.4	0.1
Fraxinus pennsylvanica	11.1	0.0
Populus deltoides ssp. monilifera	11.1	0.2
unknown tree - hardwood	22.2	0.1
TOTAL	166.7	0.7

Plot: 5086

Species	Density (individuals / ha)	Basal Area (m²/ ha)
hardwood		
Acer saccharinum	22.2	0.3
Populus deltoides ssp. monilifera	11.1	0.9
unknown tree - hardwood	44.4	3.5
TOTAL	77.8	4.7

Plot: 5096

Species	Density (individuals / ha)	Basal Area (m²/ ha)
hardwood		
Prunus serotina	11.1	0.1
TOTAL	11.1	0.1

Plot: 5097

Species	Density (individuals / ha)	Basal Area (m²/ ha)
hardwood		
Acer negundo	11.1	0.0
Fraxinus pennsylvanica	11.1	0.5
Tilia americana	11.1	0.0
unknown tree - hardwood	200.0	3.9
TOTAL	233.3	4.4

Plot: 5099

Species	Density (individuals / ha)	Basal Area (m²/ ha)
hardwood		
Acer saccharinum	11.1	1.9
Populus deltoides ssp. monilifera	11.1	3.5
unknown tree - hardwood	22.2	1.4
TOTAL	44.4	6.8

Plot: 5104

Species	Density (individuals / ha)	Basal Area (m²/ ha)
hardwood		
Fraxinus pennsylvanica	24.7	0.0
Populus deltoides ssp. monilifera	12.3	6.4
unknown tree - hardwood	12.3	0.6
TOTAL	**49.4**	**7.0**

Plot: 5106

Species	Density (individuals / ha)	Basal Area (m²/ ha)
hardwood		
Acer saccharinum	22.2	1.2
Ulmus rubra	11.1	0.6
TOTAL	**33.3**	**1.8**

Plot: 5111

Species	Density (individuals / ha)	Basal Area (m²/ ha)
hardwood		
Acer negundo	11.1	0.3
Acer saccharinum	22.2	0.5
TOTAL	**33.3**	**0.9**

Plot: 5140

Species	Density (individuals / ha)	Basal Area (m²/ ha)
hardwood		
Acer negundo	11.1	0.0
Fraxinus pennsylvanica	55.6	0.3
unknown tree - hardwood	55.6	0.4
TOTAL	**122.2**	**0.8**

Plot: 5142

Species	Density (individuals / ha)	Basal Area (m²/ ha)
hardwood		
Acer saccharinum	22.2	0.8
TOTAL	**22.2**	**0.8**

Plot: 5148

Species	Density (individuals / ha)	Basal Area (m²/ ha)
hardwood		
Acer negundo	11.1	1.2
unknown tree - hardwood	33.3	0.5
TOTAL	**44.4**	**1.7**

Percent Cover of Shrub Species

Plot: 5002

Species	1	2	3	4	5	6	mean percent cover
Cornus alternifolia	1	1	1		1	1	0.83
Lonicera morrowii	30			1	2		5.50
Menispermum canadense	1			4	1		1.00
Parthenocissus sp.	1	1	1	4	1	1	1.50
Rhamnus cathartica	4	4	4	4	2	2	3.33
R bes hirtellum	20	10	4	8	2	2	7.67
Rubus occidentalis	1						0.17
Rubus pensilvanicus	1				1	1	0.50
Rubus pubescens		1	1	1			0.50
Sambucus racemosa var. racemosa	10	4	4		3	2	3.83
Smilax tamnoides	4	1	1	1	1	1	1.50

Number of Shrub Circles Not Sampled in Plot 5002: 0

Plot: 5004

Species	1	2	3	4	5	6	mean percent cover
Parthenocissus sp.	25	2		1			4.67
Rhamnus cathartica	10	5		5			3.33
R bes hirtellum	5	1					1.00
Rubus occidentalis				15			2.50
Vitis riparia	1	1		1			0.50

Number of Shrub Circles Not Sampled in Plot 5004: 0

Plot: 5006

Species	1	2	3	4	5	6	mean percent cover
Euonymus atropurpurea	1	1					0.33
Lonicera (exotic) sp.	1				1	1	0.50
Lonicera sp.			1	1			0.33
Menispermum canadense		1	4			1	1.00
Parthenocissus sp.	1	1	30	40	1	1	12.33
Rhamnus cathartica	2	1	10	15	50	30	18.00
R bes cynosbati					1	1	0.33
R bes hirtellum	2		1	1	1		0.83
Rubus idaeus ssp. strigosus					1		0.17
Rubus occidentalis				1			0.17
Rubus pubescens						1	0.17
Smilax tamnoides				1			0.17
Solanum dulcamara	1	1					0.33
Vitis riparia	1	2			1		0.67
Zanthoxylum americanum					1	1	0.33

Number of Shrub Circles Not Sampled in Plot 5006: 0

Plot: 5010

Species	Percent cover in shrub circles						mean percent cover
	1	**2**	**3**	**4**	**5**	**6**	
Menispermum canadense	1	1	1		1	1	0.83
Sambucus nigra ssp. canadensis				4		1	0.83
Smilax tamnoides			1				0.17

Number of Shrub Circles Not Sampled in Plot 5010: 0

Plot: 5016

Species	Percent cover in shrub circles						mean percent cover
	1	**2**	**3**	**4**	**5**	**6**	
Euonymus atropurpurea					2		0.33
Parthenocissus sp.	3	1	5	5	3	1	3.00
Rhamnus cathartica	2	10	5	1	1	1	3.33
R bes hirtellum	5	15	1	5	2		4.67
Rubus occidentalis		1		5	5	1	2.00
Smilax tamnoides	1	1				1	0.50
Solanum dulcamara	1						0.17
Viburnum opulus var. americanum		1	1				0.33
Vitis riparia	1	1	15	15	15	1	8.00
Zanthoxylum americanum	1	5	3		10		3.17

Number of Shrub Circles Not Sampled in Plot 5016: 0

Plot: 5018

Species	Percent cover in shrub circles						mean percent cover
	1	**2**	**3**	**4**	**5**	**6**	
Cornus alternifolia	1		1	1	1	1	0.83
Cornus racemosa	1	1			1	2	0.83
Corylus americana					1	1	0.33
Lonicera (exotic) sp.	40	30	10	25	20	15	23.33
Parthenocissus sp.	5	1	1	1	1	1	1.67
Rhamnus cathartica	10	5	1		1	1	3.00
R bes cynosbati		5					0.83
R bes hirtellum		5	1	1	1	1	1.50
Rosa carolina	1						0.17
Rubus idaeus ssp. strigosus	1	5					1.00
Rubus occidentalis			1				0.17
Rubus setosus	1						0.17
Smilax tamnoides	1		1				0.33
Toxicodendron radicans	5					1	1.00
Viburnum rafinesqueanum		1					0.17
Vitis riparia	1	1				1	0.50
Zanthoxylum americanum	10					1	1.83

Number of Shrub Circles Not Sampled in Plot 5018: 0

Plot: 5020

Species	\multicolumn{6}{c}{Percent cover in shrub circles}	mean percent cover
	1	2	3	4	5	6	
Acer ginnala	1					1	0.33
Cornus sericea	2	5	4	4	2	12	4.83
Lonicera (exotic) sp.			1	4		4	1.50
Menispermum canadense			1				0.17
Parthenocissus sp.	2	3	10	5	10	4	5.67
Physocarpus opulifolius						1	0.17
Rhamnus cathartica	1	1	10	20	1	50	13.83
R bes americanum				12	1	5	3.00
R bes hirtellum					4		0.67
Rubus idaeus ssp. strigosus	1						0.17
Rubus occidentalis			4		4	4	2.00
Rubus pubescens						1	0.17
Solanum dulcamara	1		1	1		1	0.67
Viburnum rafinesqueanum				1			0.17
Vitis riparia	1	2	5	5	1	1	2.50

Number of Shrub Circles Not Sampled in Plot 5020: 0

Plot: 5021

Species	\multicolumn{6}{c}{Percent cover in shrub circles}	mean percent cover
	1	2	3	4	5	6	
Menispermum canadense	1						0.17
Rhamnus cathartica	1						0.17
Vitis riparia			1				0.17

Number of Shrub Circles Not Sampled in Plot 5021: 0

Plot: 5022

Species	\multicolumn{6}{c}{Percent cover in shrub circles}	mean percent cover
	1	2	3	4	5	6	
Rhamnus cathartica	1			1	1	1	0.67
Vitis riparia	1	1		1	1	1	0.83

Number of Shrub Circles Not Sampled in Plot 5022: 0

Plot: 5031

Species	\multicolumn{6}{c}{Percent cover in shrub circles}	mean percent cover
	1	2	3	4	5	6	
Cornus racemosa				1			0.17
Lonicera (exotic) sp.	1			1			0.33
Parthenocissus sp.	2	1	1	1	2	1	1.33
Rhamnus cathartica	50	50	50	15	45	30	40.00
R bes hirtellum	1	1	1	1	1	1	1.00
Rubus occidentalis		1		1	1		0.50
Vitis riparia		1	1		1	1	0.67
Zanthoxylum americanum	1	1	1				0.50

Number of Shrub Circles Not Sampled in Plot 5031: 0

Plot: 5033

Species	1	2	3	4	5	6	mean percent cover
Lonicera (exotic) sp.	8		1	15	1	1	4.33
Menispermum canadense			1				0.17
Parthenocissus sp.	1	4	1	1	1		1.33
Rhamnus cathartica	10	8	30		20	25	15.50
R bes hirtellum	4	12	1	1		1	3.17
Rubus occidentalis	1	4		1			1.00
Rubus pubescens	1						0.17
Toxicodendron rydbergii	1						0.17
Vitis riparia	1	1	1	2		1	1.00
Zanthoxylum americanum	1						0.17

Number of Shrub Circles Not Sampled in Plot 5033: 0

Plot: 5034

Species	1	2	3	4	5	6	mean percent cover
Rhamnus cathartica		1					0.17
Sambucus nigra ssp. canadensis	3		1				0.67
Vitis riparia	1	2	1		1		0.83
Zanthoxylum americanum	3	4					1.17

Number of Shrub Circles Not Sampled in Plot 5034: 0

Plot: 5035

Species	1	2	3	4	5	6	mean percent cover
Menispermum canadense		5					0.83
Parthenocissus sp.	1	4					0.83
Rhamnus cathartica		1					0.17
R bes cynosbati		1					0.17
Sambucus sp.		1					0.17
Smilax tamnoides	4	5					1.50
Vitis riparia	1					1	0.33

Number of Shrub Circles Not Sampled in Plot 5035: 0

Plot: 5038

Species	1	2	3	4	5	6	mean percent cover
Rhamnus cathartica		1					0.17
Sambucus nigra ssp. canadensis					2		0.33
Vitis riparia		1					0.17

Number of Shrub Circles Not Sampled in Plot 5038: 0

Plot: 5039

Species	\multicolumn{6}{c}{Percent cover in shrub circles}						mean percent cover
	1	2	3	4	5	6	
Cornus alternifolia	1	1				1	0.50
Cornus racemosa						1	0.17
Lonicera (exotic) sp.	2	1					0.50
Parthenocissus quinquefolia	1	1	1				0.50
Parthenocissus sp.				2	1	1	0.67
Rhamnus cathartica	2	1	1	2		1	1.17
R bes hirtellum	2		2	2	1	1	1.33
R bes sp.		3					0.50
Rubus occidentalis	2	2	1	2			1.17
Smilax tamnoides	1	1					0.33
Toxicodendron radicans	1	1					0.33
Vitis riparia	1	1	1	1	1		0.83

Number of Shrub Circles Not Sampled in Plot 5039: 0

Plot: 5042

Species	\multicolumn{6}{c}{Percent cover in shrub circles}						mean percent cover
	1	2	3	4	5	6	
Menispermum canadense					1		0.17
Sambucus nigra ssp. canadensis		1					0.17
Smilax tamnoides	2						0.33
Toxicodendron radicans	2						0.33

Number of Shrub Circles Not Sampled in Plot 5042: 0

Plot: 5052

Species	\multicolumn{6}{c}{Percent cover in shrub circles}						mean percent cover
	1	2	3	4	5	6	
Rhamnus cathartica	1	1					0.50
Smilax tamnoides	1						0.25
Vitis riparia		1		1			0.50

Number of Shrub Circles Not Sampled in Plot 5052: 2

Plot: 5056

Species	\multicolumn{6}{c}{Percent cover in shrub circles}						mean percent cover
	1	2	3	4	5	6	
Parthenocissus sp.	1	1	1			1	0.67
Rhamnus cathartica	1	1	4	1		1	1.33
Rubus occidentalis	1	4					0.83
Rubus pubescens				1		1	0.33
Vitis riparia	3	1	2		5	1	2.00

Number of Shrub Circles Not Sampled in Plot 5056: 0

Plot: 5073

Species	1	2	3	4	5	6	mean percent cover
Lonicera (exotic) sp.	25		3	5	10		7.17
Menispermum canadense		1					0.17
Parthenocissus sp.	1	1	2	1	2	1	1.33
Rhamnus cathartica	1	1	1	1	1	1	1.00
R bes hirtellum	1	1	1	1	1		0.83
Rubus occidentalis	1						0.17
Rubus pensilvanicus		1				1	0.33
Rubus pubescens				1			0.17
Smilax tamnoides	1	1	1			1	0.67
Vitis riparia	1	1	1	1	1		0.83
Zanthoxylum americanum				1			0.17

Number of Shrub Circles Not Sampled in Plot 5073: 0

Plot: 5076

Species	1	2	3	4	5	6	mean percent cover
Humulus lupulus	1						0.17
Menispermum canadense	1			4			0.83
Parthenocissus sp.	1		20	4		1	4.33
Rhamnus cathartica	1		1	1	1	1	0.83
R bes americanum			1	4			0.83
Vitis riparia	1			1	1		0.50

Number of Shrub Circles Not Sampled in Plot 5076: 0

Plot: 5082

Species	1	2	3	4	5	6	mean percent cover
Berberis vulgaris			3				0.50
Cornus alternifolia					1		0.17
Lonicera (exotic) sp.	30		25	25	20	5	17.50
Menispermum canadense		1					0.17
Parthenocissus sp.	1	5	1		1	1	1.50
Rhamnus cathartica	20	25	20	10	15	50	23.33
R bes cynosbati	1	1	1		1	1	0.83
R bes hirtellum	1	1			1	1	0.67
Rubus idaeus ssp. strigosus		2					0.33
Sambucus nigra ssp. canadensis		2					0.33
Solanum dulcamara		1					0.17
Toxicodendron radicans			1				0.17
Viburnum sp.				1			0.17
Vitis riparia	1	1	1				0.50
Zanthoxylum americanum			1				0.17

Number of Shrub Circles Not Sampled in Plot 5082: 0

Plot: 5084

Species	Percent cover in shrub circles						mean percent cover
	1	2	3	4	5	6	
Parthenocissus sp.				1		1	0.33
Vitis riparia	1		1	1	1		0.67

Number of Shrub Circles Not Sampled in Plot 5084: 0

Plot: 5086

Species	Percent cover in shrub circles						mean percent cover
	1	2	3	4	5	6	
R bes americanum				1			0.17
Sambucus nigra ssp. canadensis			1				0.17
Solanum dulcamara		1					0.17
Vitis riparia	1	1	1	1	1		0.83

Number of Shrub Circles Not Sampled in Plot 5086: 0

Plot: 5096

Species	Percent cover in shrub circles						mean percent cover
	1	2	3	4	5	6	
Menispermum canadense		1					0.17
Parthenocissus sp.	1	1	1	1	4	1	1.50
Physocarpus opulifolius		1					0.17
Rhamnus cathartica	10	20	40	20	35	20	24.17
R bes hirtellum	5	5	8	1	5	4	4.67
Rubus idaeus ssp. strigosus	1						0.17
Rubus occidentalis					1	1	0.33
Rubus pubescens	1	1	1	1	1	1	1.00
Sambucus sp.			1	1			0.33
Toxicodendron rydbergii	1		1				0.33
Vitis riparia	1	1					0.33
Zanthoxylum americanum	1				1		0.33

Number of Shrub Circles Not Sampled in Plot 5096: 0

Plot: 5097

Species	Percent cover in shrub circles						mean percent cover
	1	2	3	4	5	6	
Cornus alternifolia		5			1		1.00
Euonymus atropurpurea					3		0.50
Lonicera (exotic) sp.						10	1.67
Menispermum canadense		5	1	1	10	5	3.67
Parthenocissus sp.	1			1		1	0.50
R bes cynosbati					1	10	1.83
R bes hirtellum		5	4	4	10	25	8.00
Sambucus racemosa var. racemosa				1			0.17
Smilax tamnoides			1				0.17
Toxicodendron radicans		1				1	0.33
Vitis riparia	1					1	0.33

Number of Shrub Circles Not Sampled in Plot 5097: 0

Plot: 5099

Species	Percent cover in shrub circles						mean percent cover
	1	2	3	4	5	6	
Menispermum canadense	1						0.17
Parthenocissus sp.	1		1				0.33
Sambucus nigra ssp. canadensis	1		1				0.33
Smilax tamnoides	1						0.17
Solanum dulcamara		1					0.17

Number of Shrub Circles Not Sampled in Plot 5099: 0

Plot: 5104

Species	Percent cover in shrub circles						mean percent cover
	1	2	3	4	5	6	
Parthenocissus sp.	1	2			1		0.67
Rhamnus cathartica	2	5		1	1		1.50
R bes hirtellum		1					0.17
Solanum dulcamara					1		0.17
Toxicodendron radicans		1					0.17
Vitis riparia	1	1		1	1	5	1.50

Number of Shrub Circles Not Sampled in Plot 5104: 0

Plot: 5106

Species	Percent cover in shrub circles						mean percent cover
	1	2	3	4	5	6	
Smilax tamnoides	1						0.17
Vitis riparia					2		0.33

Number of Shrub Circles Not Sampled in Plot 5106: 0

Plot: 5111

Species	Percent cover in shrub circles						mean percent cover
	1	2	3	4	5	6	
Rhamnus cathartica					1		0.17
Vitis riparia			1		15		2.67

Number of Shrub Circles Not Sampled in Plot 5111: 0

Plot: 5140

Species	Percent cover in shrub circles						mean percent cover
	1	2	3	4	5	6	
Cornus alternifolia			2		1	10	2.17
Euonymus atropurpurea			1	1			0.33
Parthenocissus sp.	5		1	2		2	1.67
Rhamnus cathartica				1	5	10	2.67
R bes hirtellum		2	1	2			0.83
Smilax tamnoides	1		1	1	1	1	0.83
Viburnum lantana				5			0.83
Viburnum lentago			10				1.67
Vitis riparia	1		1				0.33

Number of Shrub Circles Not Sampled in Plot 5140: 0

Plot: 5142

Species	Percent cover in shrub circles 1	2	3	4	5	6	mean percent cover
Menispermum canadense			1				0.17
Sambucus nigra ssp. canadensis	2		1				0.50
Vitis riparia						1	0.17

Number of Shrub Circles Not Sampled in Plot 5142: 0

Plot: 5148

Species	Percent cover in shrub circles 1	2	3	4	5	6	mean percent cover
Parthenocissus sp.		5	2	1			1.33
Rhamnus cathartica	10	35	1		1		7.83
R bes americanum			2				0.33
R bes hirtellum	10	1	20				5.17
Rubus occidentalis		1					0.17
Sambucus nigra ssp. canadensis			1				0.17
Solanum dulcamara		1					0.17
Vitis riparia	1	1					0.33

Number of Shrub Circles Not Sampled in Plot 5148: 0

Frequency of Species in Groundlayer Quadrats

Plot: 5002

Species	Quadrat Frequency Transect 1	2	3	Mean Quadrat Frequency
Acer negundo	0.4	0.1	0.1	0.20
Anemone quinquefolia	0.0	0.0	0.3	0.10
Arisaema triphyllum	0.7	0.9	0.6	0.73
Athyrium filix-femina ssp. angustum	0.0	0.0	0.2	0.07
Boehmeria cylindrica	0.1	0.0	0.0	0.03
Caltha palustris	0.0	0.0	0.1	0.03
Carex blanda	0.3	0.3	0.1	0.23
Carex pedunculata	0.2	0.1	0.1	0.13
Carex radiata	0.1	0.1	0.0	0.07
Carex sp.	0.0	0.1	0.1	0.07
Carya cordiformis	0.1	0.4	0.8	0.43
Caulophyllum thalictroides	0.2	0.0	0.1	0.10
Celtis occidentalis	0.6	0.3	0.1	0.33
Circaea lutetiana ssp. canadensis	1	0.9	1	0.97
Cornus alternifolia	0.0	0.0	0.1	0.03
Cystopteris fragilis	0.0	0.0	0.1	0.03
Fraxinus pennsylvanica	0.2	0.1	0.3	0.20
Galium aparine	1	1	1	1.00
Galium triflorum	0.0	0.0	0.3	0.10
Geranium maculatum	0.2	0.8	0.7	0.57
Geum sp.	0.4	0.3	0.7	0.47
Hydrophyllum virginianum	0.0	0.7	0.2	0.30
Impatiens sp.	0.2	0.0	0.0	0.07
Lonicera morrowii	0.6	0.2	0.0	0.27
Maianthemum canadense	1	0.0	0.3	0.43
Menispermum canadense	0.0	0.3	0.0	0.10
Osmorhiza claytonii	0.4	0.0	0.0	0.13
Parthenocissus sp.	0.3	0.5	0.4	0.40
Polygonatum biflorum	0.3	0.0	0.0	0.10
Prunus serotina	0.3	0.0	0.0	0.10
Prunus virginiana	0.1	0.0	0.2	0.10
Rhamnus cathartica	0.6	0.5	0.4	0.50
R bes cynosbati	0.0	0.0	0.3	0.10
R bes hirtellum	0.9	0.8	0.6	0.77
Rubus occidentalis	0.0	0.0	0.1	0.03
Rubus pubescens	0.0	0.1	0.0	0.03
Sambucus nigra ssp. canadensis	0.0	0.0	0.2	0.07
Sambucus racemosa var. racemosa	0.2	0.0	0.0	0.07
Sanguinaria canadensis	0.2	0.1	0.1	0.13
Sanicula sp.	0.0	0.5	0.0	0.17
Smilax tamnoides	0.0	0.0	0.1	0.03
Solidago sp.	0.3	0.2	0.0	0.17
Streptopus lanceolatus var. roseus	0.0	0.0	0.1	0.03
Thalictrum dioicum	0.0	0.0	0.2	0.07
Ulmus rubra	0.5	0.1	0.2	0.27
Viola pubescens	0.0	0.7	0.0	0.23
Viola sp.	0.5	0.0	0.9	0.47

Plot: 5004

Species	Quadrat Frequency Transect 1	2	3	Mean Quadrat Frequency
Acer negundo	0.2	0.0	0.0	0.07
Alliaria petiolata	1	0.2	0.0	0.40
Arctium minus	0.3	0.2	0.0	0.17
Cardamine pensylvanica	0.1	0.1	0.1	0.10
Carex sp.	0.1	0.0	0.0	0.03
Celtis occidentalis	0.1	0.0	0.0	0.03
Circaea lutetiana ssp. canadensis	0.1	0.0	0.0	0.03
Fraxinus pennsylvanica	0.1	0.0	0.0	0.03
Galium triflorum	0.1	0.0	0.0	0.03
Geum sp.	0.2	0.0	0.0	0.07
Impatiens sp.	0.3	0.0	0.0	0.10
Laportea canadensis	0.2	0.5	0.9	0.53
Lemna minor	0.0	0.5	0.0	0.17
Parthenocissus sp.	0.6	0.2	0.0	0.27
Phalaris arundinacea	0.0	0.2	0.0	0.07
Poaceae fam.	0.0	0.0	0.1	0.03
Rhamnus cathartica	0.8	0.1	0.0	0.30
Rubus occidentalis	0.0	0.1	0.0	0.03
Sanguinaria canadensis	0.2	0.0	0.0	0.07
Solidago sp.	0.2	0.3	0.0	0.17
Stachys tenuifolia	0.0	0.2	0.0	0.07
Taraxacum officinale	0.1	0.0	0.0	0.03
Viola sp.	0.2	0.0	0.0	0.07
Vitis riparia	0.4	0.0	0.0	0.13

Plot: 5006

Species	Quadrat Frequency Transect 1	2	3	Mean Quadrat Frequency
Acer saccharum	0.0	0.1	0.1	0.07
Carex assiniboinensis	0.3	0.0	0.0	0.10
Carex blanda	0.1	0.0	0.3	0.13
Carex pensylvanica	0.0	0.1	0.0	0.03
Carya cordiformis	0.0	0.3	0.0	0.10
Cerastium fontanum ssp. vulgare	0.0	0.0	0.1	0.03
Circaea lutetiana ssp. canadensis	0.1	0.1	0.0	0.07
Clematis virginiana	0.0	0.0	0.1	0.03
Erigeron sp.	0.0	0.0	0.1	0.03
Euonymus atropurpurea	0.3	0.0	0.0	0.10
Fragaria vesca	0.0	0.0	0.1	0.03
Fragaria virginiana	0.0	0.4	0.4	0.27
Fraxinus nigra	0.0	0.0	0.1	0.03
Fraxinus pennsylvanica	0.7	0.0	0.2	0.30
Galium aparine	0.0	0.2	0.0	0.07
Galium asprellum	0.4	0.0	0.0	0.13
Galium trifidum	0.0	0.0	0.2	0.07
Galium triflorum	0.0	0.1	0.0	0.03
Geranium maculatum	0.0	0.0	0.1	0.03
Geum laciniatum	0.0	0.2	0.0	0.07
Geum sp.	0.1	0.0	0.0	0.03
Hydrophyllum virginianum	0.1	0.4	0.1	0.20
Laportea canadensis	0.2	0.0	0.0	0.07
Lonicera (exotic) sp.	0.0	0.4	0.0	0.13
Medicago lupulina	0.0	0.0	0.2	0.07
Menispermum canadense	0.1	0.0	0.0	0.03
Parthenocissus sp.	0.7	1	0.3	0.67
Poa compressa	0.0	0.0	0.4	0.13
Polygonatum biflorum	0.0	0.0	0.1	0.03
Prunus pensylvanica	0.0	0.3	0.0	0.10
Prunus virginiana	0.0	0.0	0.1	0.03
Rhamnus cathartica	0.9	1	1	0.97
R bes hirtellum	0.6	0.6	0.4	0.53
Rubus idaeus ssp. strigosus	0.1	0.1	0.1	0.10
Rubus occidentalis	0.2	0.0	0.3	0.17
Sambucus nigra ssp. canadensis	0.1	0.0	0.0	0.03
Sicyos angulatus	0.5	0.0	0.1	0.20
Smilax tamnoides	0.1	0.0	0.0	0.03
Solidago sp.	0.1	0.1	0.0	0.07
Streptopus lanceolatus var. roseus	0.0	0.0	0.1	0.03
Taraxacum officinale	0.0	0.4	0.3	0.23
Tilia americana	0.0	0.1	0.1	0.07
Verbascum thapsus	0.0	0.0	0.2	0.07
Viola sp.	0.2	0.0	0.3	0.17
Vitis riparia	0.2	0.5	0.3	0.33
Zanthoxylum americanum	0.1	0.0	0.0	0.03

Plot: 5010

Species	Quadrat Frequency Transect 1	2	3	Mean Quadrat Frequency
Arctium minus	0.0	0.0	0.2	0.07
Bidens cernua	0.0	0.1	0.0	0.03
Boehmeria cylindrica	0.0	0.0	0.1	0.03
Impatiens sp.	0.0	0.2	0.0	0.07
Laportea canadensis	0.4	0.9	0.7	0.67
Menispermum canadense	0.0	0.0	0.2	0.07
Phalaris arundinacea	0.4	0.0	0.7	0.37
Ranunculus sp.	0.0	0.0	0.1	0.03
Rudbeckia laciniata	0.0	0.0	0.1	0.03
Rumex sp.	0.0	0.0	0.1	0.03
Sanicula sp.	0.0	0.0	0.2	0.07
Scutellaria sp.	0.4	0.0	0.1	0.17
Smilax tamnoides	0.0	0.1	0.0	0.03
Solanum dulcamara	0.1	0.0	0.0	0.03
Solidago sp.	0.3	0.1	0.1	0.17
Ulmus rubra	0.1	0.0	0.0	0.03
Urtica dioica ssp. gracilis	0.1	0.0	0.0	0.03

Plot: 5016

| Species | Quadrat Frequency | | | Mean Quadrat Frequency |
| | Transect | | | |
	1	2	3	
Alliaria petiolata	0.1	0.3	0.0	0.13
Amphicarpaea bracteata	0.0	0.1	0.0	0.03
Boehmeria cylindrica	0.3	0.0	0.0	0.10
Bromus inermis	0.1	0.0	0.0	0.03
Carex blanda	0.1	0.0	0.0	0.03
Carex grisea	0.2	0.0	0.0	0.07
Carex sp.	0.0	0.3	0.0	0.10
Celtis occidentalis	0.2	0.6	0.1	0.30
Circaea lutetiana ssp. canadensis	0.4	0.0	0.0	0.13
Cryptotaenia canadensis	0.2	0.4	0.0	0.20
Elymus sp.	0.1	0.0	0.0	0.03
Elymus virginicus	0.0	0.4	0.0	0.13
Fraxinus nigra	0.0	0.0	0.1	0.03
Fraxinus pennsylvanica	0.2	0.0	0.1	0.10
Galium aparine	0.6	0.3	0.1	0.33
Galium triflorum	0.1	0.0	0.0	0.03
Geum sp.	0.1	0.0	0.0	0.03
Glechoma hederacea	0.8	1	0.6	0.80
Hackelia virginiana	0.1	0.1	0.1	0.10
Heracleum sphondylium ssp. montanum	0.0	0.7	0.1	0.27
Hydrophyllum virginianum	0.4	0.1	0.1	0.20
Impatiens sp.	0.2	0.3	0.1	0.20
Laportea canadensis	0.8	1	0.5	0.77
Leonurus cardiaca	0.1	0.0	0.0	0.03
Lysimachia ciliata	0.0	0.1	0.0	0.03
Oxalis sp.	0.2	0.0	0.0	0.07
Parthenocissus sp.	0.2	1	0.5	0.57
Phalaris arundinacea	0.1	0.0	0.0	0.03
Pilea sp.	0.2	0.4	0.0	0.20
Plantago major	0.0	0.0	0.1	0.03
Plantago rugelii	0.2	0.0	0.1	0.10
Poa compressa	0.0	0.0	0.2	0.07
Poa pratensis	0.3	0.0	0.3	0.20
Poaceae fam.	0.0	0.0	0.1	0.03
Polygonatum biflorum	0.2	0.0	0.3	0.17
Prunus serotina	0.1	0.0	0.0	0.03
Prunus virginiana	0.0	0.0	0.1	0.03
Ranunculus abortivus	0.0	0.0	0.1	0.03
Ranunculus sceleratus	0.1	0.0	0.0	0.03
Rhamnus cathartica	0.6	0.3	0.5	0.47
R bes hirtellum	0.7	0.1	0.4	0.40
Rubus occidentalis	0.3	0.3	0.1	0.23
Solidago sp.	0.4	0.4	0.3	0.37
Stachys tenuifolia	0.0	0.3	0.2	0.17
Taraxacum officinale	0.2	0.0	0.3	0.17
Viola sp.	0.2	0.1	0.4	0.23
Vitis riparia	0.5	0.6	0.2	0.43
Zanthoxylum americanum	0.1	0.0	0.4	0.17

Plot: 5018

| Species | Quadrat Frequency | | | Mean Quadrat Frequency |
| | Transect | | | |
	1	2	3	
Actaea sp.	0.0	0.1	0.0	0.03
Arisaema triphyllum	0.0	0.0	0.1	0.03
Asteraceae fam.	0.1	0.0	0.0	0.03
Betula sp.	0.1	0.1	0.0	0.07
Botrychium sp.	0.1	0.0	0.0	0.03
Bromus inermis	0.1	0.0	0.0	0.03
Carex blanda	0.1	0.1	0.0	0.07
Carex pensylvanica	0.2	0.1	0.1	0.13
Carya cordiformis	0.3	0.1	0.1	0.17
Caulophyllum thalictroides	0.0	0.0	0.1	0.03
Cerastium sp.	0.1	0.0	0.0	0.03
Circaea lutetiana ssp. canadensis	0.1	0.1	0.1	0.10
Cornus alternifolia	0.1	0.0	0.1	0.07
Cornus racemosa	0.4	0.1	0.0	0.17
Corylus americana	0.0	0.0	0.1	0.03
Desmodium sp.	0.0	0.0	0.2	0.07
Equisetum hyemale	0.0	0.3	0.2	0.17
Equisetum pratense	0.0	0.1	0.0	0.03
Erigeron philadelphicus	0.0	0.1	0.0	0.03
Eurybia macrophylla	0.5	0.4	0.3	0.40
Fragaria virginiana	0.0	0.0	0.2	0.07
Fraxinus pennsylvanica	0.3	0.0	0.1	0.13
Galium triflorum	0.2	0.1	0.2	0.17
Geranium maculatum	0.4	0.0	0.0	0.13
Hydrophyllum virginianum	0.1	0.1	0.0	0.07
Juniperus virginiana	0.0	0.0	0.2	0.07
Lonicera (exotic) sp.	0.6	0.7	0.8	0.70
Maianthemum racemosum	0.0	0.1	0.0	0.03
Maianthemum stellatum	0.0	0.0	0.1	0.03
Orchidaceae fam.	0.1	0.0	0.0	0.03
Osmorhiza claytonii	0.0	0.0	0.1	0.03
Ostrya virginiana	0.5	0.1	0.1	0.23
Oxalis sp.	0.0	0.1	0.0	0.03
Parthenocissus sp.	0.5	0.6	0.8	0.63
Plantago rugelii	0.1	0.1	0.1	0.10
Poa compressa	0.2	0.0	0.1	0.10
Poa sp.	0.0	0.1	0.1	0.07
Polygonatum biflorum	0.2	0.1	0.1	0.13
Populus tremuloides	0.0	0.1	0.0	0.03
Potentilla anserina ssp. anserina	0.0	0.0	0.2	0.07
Prunus pensylvanica	0.0	0.2	0.1	0.10
Prunus sp.	0.0	0.0	0.1	0.03
Prunus virginiana	0.1	0.1	0.1	0.10
Quercus rubra	0.2	0.0	0.0	0.07
Rhamnus cathartica	0.2	0.2	0.5	0.30
Ribes hirtellum	0.1	0.2	0.1	0.13
Rubus occidentalis	0.1	0.0	0.0	0.03
Sanguinaria canadensis	0.7	0.1	0.0	0.27
Smilax sp.	0.0	0.2	0.0	0.07
Smilax tamnoides	0.2	0.1	0.3	0.20
Solidago sp.	0.1	0.1	0.0	0.07
Taraxacum officinale	0.1	0.2	0.1	0.13
Tilia americana	0.2	0.1	0.0	0.10
Toxicodendron radicans	0.4	0.1	0.0	0.17
Trifolium pratense	0.1	0.0	0.0	0.03
Trifolium repens	0.0	0.0	0.1	0.03
Ulmus rubra	0.2	0.0	0.0	0.07

Plot: 5018

| Species | Quadrat Frequency | | | Mean Quadrat Frequency |
| | Transect | | | |
	1	2	3	
Uvularia grandiflora	0.0	0.2	0.0	0.07
Verbascum thapsus	0.0	0.0	0.1	0.03
Vitis riparia	0.3	0.0	0.3	0.20
Zanthoxylum americanum	0.1	0.2	0.2	0.17

Plot: 5020

| Species | Quadrat Frequency | | | Mean Quadrat Frequency |
| | Transect | | | |
	1	2	3	
Acer negundo	0.4	0.2	0.1	0.23
Actaea rubra	0.0	0.0	0.1	0.03
Alliaria petiolata	0.0	0.0	0.1	0.03
Amphicarpaea bracteata	0.0	0.5	0.2	0.23
Arisaema triphyllum	0.1	0.5	0.5	0.37
Boehmeria cylindrica	0.6	0.0	0.1	0.23
Carex blanda	0.3	0.1	0.6	0.33
Carex grisea	0.0	0.0	0.1	0.03
Carex stipata	0.1	0.0	0.0	0.03
Celtis occidentalis	0.1	0.2	0.2	0.17
Circaea lutetiana ssp. canadensis	0.2	0.5	0.7	0.47
Cornus amomum	0.6	0.0	0.0	0.20
Cornus sericea	0.0	0.1	0.0	0.03
Daucus carota	0.0	0.2	0.0	0.07
Equisetum arvense	0.4	0.1	0.5	0.33
Fraxinus nigra	0.2	1	0.8	0.67
Fraxinus pennsylvanica	0.8	0.6	0.3	0.57
Geranium maculatum	0.0	0.0	0.4	0.13
Geum aleppicum	0.4	0.2	0.6	0.40
Hesperis matronalis	0.0	0.0	0.1	0.03
Hydrophyllum virginianum	0.0	0.6	0.8	0.47
Impatiens sp.	0.8	0.8	0.1	0.57
Laportea canadensis	0.0	0.0	0.2	0.07
Leersia oryzoides	0.2	0.4	0.1	0.23
Lonicera (exotic) sp.	0.0	0.0	0.1	0.03
Lycopus uniflorus	0.1	0.0	0.0	0.03
Maianthemum racemosum	0.0	0.0	0.2	0.07
Maianthemum stellatum	0.0	0.0	0.3	0.10
Menispermum canadense	0.0	0.1	0.0	0.03
Oxalis stricta	0.0	0.1	0.0	0.03
Parthenocissus sp.	0.6	0.6	0.6	0.60
Phalaris arundinacea	1	0.1	0.0	0.37
Plantago major	0.0	0.0	0.1	0.03
Poaceae fam.	0.0	0.2	0.0	0.07
Prunus virginiana	0.0	0.0	0.2	0.07
Rhamnus cathartica	0.2	0.6	1	0.60
Ribes americanum	0.0	0.1	0.4	0.17
Ribes hirtellum	0.0	0.0	0.1	0.03
Sanguinaria canadensis	0.0	0.0	0.2	0.07
Smilax tamnoides	0.0	0.0	0.2	0.07
Solidago sp.	0.4	0.3	0.5	0.40
Taraxacum officinale	0.0	0.0	0.1	0.03
Tilia americana	0.0	0.1	0.1	0.07
Ulmus rubra	0.1	0.1	0.0	0.07
Viburnum lentago	0.0	0.1	0.1	0.07
Viola sp.	0.1	0.0	0.0	0.03
Vitis riparia	0.5	0.8	0.2	0.50

Plot: 5021

| Species | Quadrat Frequency | | | Mean Quadrat Frequency |
| | Transect | | | |
	1	2	3	
Arctium minus	0.1	0.0	0.0	0.03
Carex sp.	0.1	0.0	0.0	0.03
Glechoma hederacea	0.1	0.0	0.1	0.07
Impatiens sp.	0.5	0.0	0.2	0.23
Laportea canadensis	0.7	0.0	0.6	0.43
Lemna minor	0.0	1	0.3	0.43
Lycopus sp.	0.0	0.0	0.1	0.03
Lysimachia ciliata	0.0	0.1	0.0	0.03
Phalaris arundinacea	0.4	0.0	0.0	0.13
Ranunculus sp.	0.1	0.0	0.0	0.03
Rhamnus cathartica	0.0	0.0	0.1	0.03
Solidago sp.	0.1	0.0	0.2	0.10
Urtica dioica ssp. gracilis	0.1	0.0	0.0	0.03
Veronica sp.	0.0	0.1	0.0	0.03
Viola sp.	0.4	0.0	0.0	0.13

Plot: 5022

| Species | Quadrat Frequency | | | Mean Quadrat Frequency |
| | Transect | | | |
	1	2	3	
Acer saccharinum	0.0	0.0	0.1	0.03
Boehmeria cylindrica	0.0	0.0	0.2	0.07
Carex sp.	0.1	0.1	0.0	0.07
Celtis occidentalis	0.1	0.0	0.1	0.07
Fraxinus pennsylvanica	0.6	0.3	0.1	0.33
Impatiens sp.	0.1	0.0	0.0	0.03
Laportea canadensis	0.8	0.6	0.1	0.50
Lemna minor	0.1	0.1	0.6	0.27
Lysimachia nummularia	0.0	0.1	0.4	0.17
Phalaris arundinacea	0.0	0.3	0.8	0.37
Rhamnus cathartica	0.0	0.0	0.2	0.07
Solidago sp.	0.3	0.0	0.7	0.33
Ulmus rubra	0.1	0.2	0.9	0.40
Viola sp.	0.2	0.2	0.2	0.20
Vitis riparia	0.6	0.5	0.8	0.63

Plot: 5030

| Species | Quadrat Frequency | | | Mean Quadrat Frequency |
| | Transect | | | |
	1	2	3	
Asteraceae fam.	0.1	0.0	0.0	0.03
Calystegia sepium	0.1	0.0	0.0	0.03
Cucurbitaceae fam.	0.3	0.1	0.0	0.13
Laportea canadensis	0.7	0.2	0.0	0.30
Phalaris arundinacea	0.4	0.7	0.0	0.37
Stachys palustris	0.1	0.1	0.0	0.07

Plot: 5031

| Species | Quadrat Frequency | | | Mean Quadrat Frequency |
| | Transect | | | |
	1	2	3	
Actaea sp.	0.1	0.0	0.0	0.03
Amelanchier Group 2 sp.	0.0	0.0	0.1	0.03
Amphicarpaea bracteata	0.1	0.0	0.1	0.07
Arctium minus	0.0	0.0	0.1	0.03
Carex pensylvanica	0.0	0.1	0.3	0.13
Carex rosea	0.0	0.0	0.1	0.03
Celtis occidentalis	0.0	0.2	0.0	0.07
Circaea lutetiana ssp. canadensis	0.7	0.6	0.7	0.67
Desmodium glutinosum	0.0	0.0	0.1	0.03
Fraxinus pennsylvanica	0.0	0.1	0.1	0.07
Galium aparine	0.1	0.0	0.0	0.03
Galium trifidum	0.1	0.3	0.2	0.20
Geum sp.	0.0	0.1	0.1	0.07
Hackelia virginiana	0.0	0.1	0.0	0.03
Lonicera (exotic) sp.	0.0	0.0	0.2	0.07
Maianthemum canadense	0.1	0.1	0.0	0.07
Oxalis stricta	0.1	0.0	0.0	0.03
Parthenocissus sp.	0.7	0.8	0.7	0.73
Pilea sp.	0.0	0.1	0.1	0.07
Plantago rugelii	0.0	0.0	0.1	0.03
Poa pratensis	0.0	0.0	0.1	0.03
Polygonatum biflorum	0.0	0.0	0.2	0.07
Populus tremuloides	0.0	0.1	0.0	0.03
Prunus serotina	0.3	0.4	0.6	0.43
Pyrola elliptica	0.0	0.1	0.0	0.03
Quercus rubra	0.0	0.0	0.1	0.03
Ranunculus abortivus	0.0	0.0	0.1	0.03
Rhamnus cathartica	1	1	1	1.00
Ribes hirtellum	0.3	0.6	0.3	0.40
Rubus occidentalis	0.1	0.1	0.1	0.10
Solidago sp.	0.0	0.3	0.1	0.13
Symphoricarpos occidentalis	0.0	0.0	0.1	0.03
Taraxacum officinale	0.0	0.0	0.1	0.03
Ulmus americana	0.0	0.0	0.1	0.03
Viola sp.	0.2	0.2	0.0	0.13
Vitis riparia	0.2	0.0	0.4	0.20
Zanthoxylum americanum	0.0	0.1	0.0	0.03

Plot: 5033

| Species | Quadrat Frequency | | | Mean Quadrat Frequency |
| | Transect | | | |
	1	2	3	
Acer negundo	0.2	0.0	0.0	0.07
Arctium minus	0.8	0.6	0.2	0.53
Arisaema triphyllum	0.2	0.0	0.0	0.07
Cannabis sativa	0.8	0.1	0.0	0.30
Carya cordiformis	0.0	0.1	0.0	0.03
Celtis occidentalis	0.3	0.5	0.0	0.27
Chenopodium album	0.1	0.1	0.0	0.07
Chenopodium simplex	0.1	0.0	0.0	0.03
Circaea lutetiana ssp. canadensis	0.3	0.7	0.1	0.37
Cirsium altissimum	0.3	0.0	0.0	0.10
Fallopia convolvulus	0.1	0.1	0.0	0.07
Galium aparine	0.4	0.4	0.0	0.27
Galium trifidum	0.2	0.4	0.1	0.23
Geum sp.	0.2	0.5	0.0	0.23
Glechoma hederacea	0.0	0.2	0.0	0.07
Hackelia virginiana	0.1	0.0	0.0	0.03
Impatiens sp.	0.4	0.0	0.0	0.13
Leonurus cardiaca	0.4	0.2	0.0	0.20
Lonicera morrowii	0.3	0.3	0.3	0.30
Nepeta cataria	0.1	0.1	0.0	0.07
Parthenocissus sp.	0.5	0.3	0.0	0.27
Pilea pumila	0.7	0.4	0.0	0.37
Poaceae fam.	0.0	0.1	0.0	0.03
Prunus serotina	0.4	0.1	0.1	0.20
Prunus virginiana	0.1	0.0	0.1	0.07
Ranunculus abortivus	0.1	0.1	0.0	0.07
Rhamnus cathartica	0.8	1	0.9	0.90
R bes hirtellum	0.6	0.6	0.2	0.47
Rubus idaeus ssp. strigosus	0.2	0.4	0.0	0.20
Sicyos angulatus	0.1	0.0	0.0	0.03
Solidago sp.	0.1	0.3	0.0	0.13
Ulmus rubra	0.1	0.1	0.0	0.07
Viola sp.	0.4	0.6	0.0	0.33
Vitis riparia	0.4	0.3	0.2	0.30

Plot: 5034

| Species | Quadrat Frequency | | | Mean Quadrat Frequency |
| | Transect | | | |
	1	2	3	
Bidens frondosa	0.1	0.0	0.0	0.03
Cicuta maculata	0.0	0.1	0.0	0.03
Impatiens sp.	0.0	0.3	0.0	0.10
Laportea canadensis	1	0.9	1	0.97
Oxalis sp.	0.1	0.0	0.0	0.03
Pilea sp.	0.3	0.1	0.0	0.13
Poaceae fam.	0.1	0.0	0.3	0.13
Rudbeckia laciniata	0.2	0.0	0.0	0.07
Sagittaria latifolia	0.1	0.0	0.0	0.03
Sambucus nigra ssp. canadensis	0.1	0.0	0.0	0.03
Sicyos angulatus	0.2	0.1	0.0	0.10
Ulmus rubra	0.1	0.0	0.0	0.03
Vitis riparia	0.1	0.0	0.3	0.13

Plot: 5035

| Species | Quadrat Frequency | | | Mean Quadrat Frequency |
| | Transect | | | |
	1	2	3	
Bidens connata	0.0	0.2	0.0	0.07
Celtis occidentalis	0.3	0.0	0.0	0.10
Fraxinus nigra	0.2	0.0	0.0	0.07
Impatiens sp.	0.1	0.0	0.1	0.07
Laportea canadensis	1	0.9	1	0.97
Lysimachia ciliata	0.1	0.0	0.0	0.03
Matteuccia struthiopteris	0.3	0.0	0.0	0.10
Menispermum canadense	0.5	0.0	0.0	0.17
Parthenocissus sp.	0.1	0.0	0.0	0.03
Poaceae fam.	0.1	0.1	0.0	0.07
Rudbeckia laciniata	0.2	0.0	0.0	0.07
Smilax tamnoides	0.2	0.0	0.0	0.07
Viola sp.	0.1	0.0	0.0	0.03

Plot: 5038

| Species | Quadrat Frequency | | | Mean Quadrat Frequency |
| | Transect | | | |
	1	2	3	
Acer negundo	0.1	0.0	0.0	0.03
Alliaria petiolata	0.1	0.0	0.0	0.03
Celtis occidentalis	0.0	0.1	0.0	0.03
Circaea lutetiana ssp. canadensis	0.0	0.2	0.0	0.07
Fraxinus pennsylvanica	0.0	0.1	0.0	0.03
Impatiens sp.	0.5	0.5	0.4	0.47
Laportea canadensis	1	1	1	1.00
Lycopus sp.	0.1	0.0	0.0	0.03
Menispermum canadense	0.4	0.1	0.0	0.17
Parthenocissus sp.	0.1	0.0	0.0	0.03
Phalaris arundinacea	0.2	0.0	0.0	0.07
Rhamnus cathartica	0.1	0.0	0.0	0.03
Rudbeckia laciniata	0.2	0.0	0.0	0.07
Sanicula sp.	0.1	0.0	0.0	0.03
Solidago sp.	0.1	0.0	0.0	0.03
Viola sp.	0.3	0.5	0.3	0.37

Plot: 5039

| Species | Quadrat Frequency | | | Mean Quadrat Frequency |
| | Transect | | | |
	1	2	3	
Alliaria petiolata	0.4	0.8	0.6	0.60
Amphicarpaea bracteata	1	0.4	0.4	0.60
Athyrium filix-femina ssp. angustum	0.0	0.1	0.0	0.03
Brachyelytrum erectum	0.0	0.1	0.0	0.03
Calamagrostis canadensis	0.0	0.0	0.1	0.03
Carex pensylvanica	0.2	0.0	0.0	0.07
Carex projecta	0.1	0.0	0.1	0.07
Carex rosea	0.0	0.1	0.0	0.03
Carex sp.	0.1	0.1	0.0	0.07
Celtis occidentalis	0.0	0.0	0.1	0.03
Circaea lutetiana ssp. canadensis	0.2	0.3	0.1	0.20
Desmodium glutinosum	0.7	0.7	0.5	0.63
Fraxinus nigra	0.0	0.0	0.2	0.07
Fraxinus pennsylvanica	0.2	0.1	0.1	0.13
Galium aparine	0.3	0.2	0.0	0.17
Galium trifidum	0.0	0.1	0.1	0.07
Galium triflorum	0.4	0.0	0.0	0.13
Geranium maculatum	0.8	0.6	0.9	0.77
Geum sp.	0.4	0.2	0.1	0.23
Hackelia virginiana	0.0	0.2	0.0	0.07
Menispermum canadense	0.0	0.1	0.0	0.03
Moehringia lateriflora	0.0	0.0	0.2	0.07
Oxalis stricta	0.0	0.0	0.1	0.03
Parthenocissus quinquefolia	0.1	0.0	0.0	0.03
Parthenocissus sp.	0.3	0.1	0.2	0.20
Pilea sp.	0.0	0.1	0.0	0.03
Poa sp.	0.1	0.0	0.0	0.03
Poaceae fam.	0.0	0.0	0.1	0.03
Populus tremuloides	0.2	0.0	0.0	0.07
Potentilla simplex	0.2	0.0	0.0	0.07
Prunus serotina	0.3	0.1	0.2	0.20
Prunus virginiana	0.1	0.2	0.0	0.10
Quercus rubra	0.1	0.1	0.0	0.07
Ranunculus abortivus	0.1	0.2	0.0	0.10
Rhamnus cathartica	0.4	0.1	0.2	0.23
R bes hirtellum	0.2	0.6	0.2	0.33
Rubus occidentalis	0.5	0.2	0.0	0.23
Rubus pensilvanicus	0.2	0.2	0.1	0.17
Solidago sp.	0.3	0.3	0.0	0.20
Thalictrum thalictroides	0.5	0.5	0.6	0.53
Toxicodendron rydbergii	0.0	0.2	0.0	0.07
Ulmus rubra	0.1	0.0	0.0	0.03
Uvularia sessilifolia	0.0	0.2	0.0	0.07
Viola sp.	0.0	0.1	0.0	0.03
Vitis riparia	0.3	0.1	0.2	0.20

Plot: 5042

| Species | Quadrat Frequency | | | Mean Quadrat Frequency |
| | Transect | | | |
	1	2	3	
Laportea canadensis	1	0.0	0.0	0.33
Rudbeckia laciniata	0.3	0.0	0.0	0.10
Viola sp.	0.1	0.0	0.0	0.03

Plot: 5052

| Species | Quadrat Frequency | | | Mean Quadrat Frequency |
| | Transect | | | |
	1	2	3	
Acer negundo	0.1	0.0	0.0	0.03
Cardamine pensylvanica	0.4	0.0	0.0	0.13
Carex grisea	0.1	0.0	0.0	0.03
Circaea lutetiana ssp. canadensis	0.6	0.0	0.0	0.20
Fraxinus pennsylvanica	0.3	0.0	0.0	0.10
Geum sp.	0.1	0.0	0.0	0.03
Laportea canadensis	0.4	0.0	0.0	0.13
Lemna minor	0.0	1	0.0	0.33
Parthenocissus sp.	0.2	0.0	0.0	0.07
Poaceae fam.	0.4	0.0	0.0	0.13
Rhamnus cathartica	0.4	0.0	0.0	0.13
Ribes americanum	0.1	0.0	0.0	0.03
Rudbeckia laciniata	0.1	0.0	0.0	0.03
Ulmus rubra	0.1	0.1	0.0	0.07
Viola sp.	0.2	0.0	0.0	0.07
Vitis riparia	0.1	0.0	0.0	0.03

Plot: 5056

| Species | Quadrat Frequency | | | Mean Quadrat Frequency |
| | Transect | | | |
	1	2	3	
Acer negundo	0.1	0.0	0.0	0.03
Alliaria petiolata	0.4	0.4	0.5	0.43
Amaranthus retroflexus	0.1	0.0	0.0	0.03
Amphicarpaea bracteata	0.0	0.1	0.0	0.03
Arctium minus	0.5	0.4	0.7	0.53
Asteraceae fam.	0.2	0.0	0.0	0.07
Cardamine impatiens	0.5	0.4	0.3	0.40
Carex sp.	0.1	0.2	0.0	0.10
Celtis occidentalis	0.1	0.2	0.0	0.10
Cryptotaenia canadensis	0.0	0.1	0.0	0.03
Fraxinus pennsylvanica	0.0	0.1	0.2	0.10
Glechoma hederacea	0.6	0.1	0.0	0.23
Impatiens sp.	0.3	0.1	0.0	0.13
Laportea canadensis	0.1	0.6	0.3	0.33
Oxalis stricta	0.0	0.1	0.0	0.03
Parthenocissus sp.	0.5	0.4	0.2	0.37
Poa sp.	0.0	0.1	0.0	0.03
Poaceae fam.	0.3	0.0	0.0	0.10
Rhamnus cathartica	0.2	0.3	0.5	0.33
Ribes americanum	0.0	0.1	0.0	0.03
Rudbeckia laciniata	0.0	0.1	0.0	0.03
Sicyos angulatus	0.0	0.0	0.2	0.07
Stachys palustris	0.1	0.0	0.0	0.03
Thalictrum dioicum	0.0	0.1	0.0	0.03
Ulmus rubra	0.0	0.1	0.0	0.03
Urtica dioica ssp. gracilis	0.0	0.0	0.2	0.07
Viola sp.	0.3	0.4	0.0	0.23
Vitis riparia	0.1	0.4	0.0	0.17

Plot: 5073

Species	Quadrat Frequency Transect 1	2	3	Mean Quadrat Frequency
Acalypha rhomboidea	0.0	0.4	0.4	0.27
Alliaria petiolata	0.3	0.2	0.2	0.23
Amphicarpaea bracteata	0.8	0.5	0.5	0.60
Calystegia sepium	0.1	0.0	0.0	0.03
Carex blanda	0.2	0.1	0.1	0.13
Carex pensylvanica	0.1	0.0	0.0	0.03
Carex radiata	0.0	0.0	0.1	0.03
Carex sprengelii	0.1	0.3	0.1	0.17
Carya cordiformis	0.5	0.0	0.1	0.20
Celtis occidentalis	0.8	0.3	0.4	0.50
Chenopodium album	0.0	0.0	0.1	0.03
Circaea lutetiana ssp. canadensis	0.7	0.9	0.4	0.67
Desmodium canadense	0.1	0.1	0.0	0.07
Fraxinus pennsylvanica	0.1	0.1	0.0	0.07
Galium aparine	0.6	0.3	0.1	0.33
Galium trifidum	0.8	0.3	0.1	0.40
Geum sp.	0.5	0.4	0.1	0.33
Gymnocladus dioicus	0.0	0.1	0.2	0.10
Hackelia virginiana	0.6	0.2	0.5	0.43
Impatiens sp.	0.1	0.0	0.0	0.03
Laportea canadensis	0.1	0.0	0.1	0.07
Lonicera (exotic) sp.	0.2	0.2	0.0	0.13
Osmorhiza claytonii	0.1	0.0	0.2	0.10
Oxalis stricta	0.0	0.1	0.1	0.07
Parthenocissus sp.	0.8	0.3	0.5	0.53
Pilea sp.	0.8	0.9	1	0.90
Poa compressa	0.1	0.0	0.0	0.03
Poaceae fam.	0.1	0.0	0.0	0.03
Polygonatum biflorum	0.0	0.0	0.1	0.03
Prunus serotina	0.5	0.0	0.3	0.27
Prunus virginiana	0.3	0.1	0.1	0.17
Rhamnus cathartica	0.6	0.2	0.2	0.33
R bes hirtellum	0.6	0.5	0.3	0.47
Rubus idaeus ssp. strigosus	0.0	0.0	0.1	0.03
Rubus occidentalis	0.0	0.1	0.0	0.03
Rubus pensilvanicus	0.5	0.0	0.0	0.17
Rubus pubescens	0.0	0.1	0.1	0.07
Rubus semisetosus	0.0	0.0	0.1	0.03
Rumex obtusifolius	0.0	0.0	0.1	0.03
Sanicula marilandica	0.2	0.1	0.0	0.10
Smilax tamnoides	0.1	0.1	0.1	0.10
Stachys palustris	1	0.6	0.5	0.70
Ulmus rubra	0.0	0.0	0.1	0.03
unknown Herbaceous species	0.1	0.0	0.0	0.03
Urtica dioica ssp. gracilis	0.1	0.0	0.0	0.03
Viola sp.	0.8	0.9	0.7	0.80
Vitis riparia	0.2	0.1	0.5	0.27

Plot: 5076

Species	Quadrat Frequency Transect 1	2	3	Mean Quadrat Frequency
Alliaria petiolata	0.7	0.6	0.2	0.50
Anemone virginiana	0.1	0.0	0.0	0.03
Arisaema triphyllum	0.0	0.0	0.1	0.03
Cardamine pensylvanica	0.2	0.1	0.0	0.10
Carex sp.	0.1	0.0	0.0	0.03
Celtis occidentalis	0.5	0.1	0.2	0.27
Chelidonium majus	0.0	0.0	0.1	0.03
Circaea lutetiana ssp. canadensis	0.1	0.2	0.0	0.10
Fraxinus pennsylvanica	0.1	0.1	0.0	0.07
Galium aparine	0.2	0.0	0.0	0.07
Glechoma hederacea	0.4	0.2	0.1	0.23
Impatiens sp.	0.2	0.6	0.0	0.27
Laportea canadensis	0.7	1	1	0.90
Leonurus cardiaca	0.1	0.0	0.0	0.03
Matteuccia struthiopteris	0.0	0.1	0.0	0.03
Menispermum canadense	0.3	0.4	0.0	0.23
Parthenocissus sp.	0.7	0.2	0.2	0.37
Phalaris arundinacea	0.1	0.0	0.0	0.03
Polygonatum biflorum	0.3	0.0	0.1	0.13
Ranunculus fascicularis	0.0	0.1	0.0	0.03
Rhamnus cathartica	0.4	0.0	0.1	0.17
Ribes americanum	0.0	0.1	0.0	0.03
Sicyos angulatus	0.0	0.2	0.0	0.07
Solidago sp.	0.1	0.0	0.0	0.03
Teucrium canadense	0.1	0.0	0.0	0.03
Thalictrum dioicum	0.2	0.0	0.0	0.07
Urtica dioica ssp. gracilis	0.1	0.0	0.0	0.03
Viola sp.	0.0	0.3	0.0	0.10
Vitis riparia	0.1	0.1	0.0	0.07

Plot: 5082

Species	Quadrat Frequency Transect 1	2	3	Mean Quadrat Frequency
Anemone quinquefolia	0.0	0.0	0.3	0.10
Carya cordiformis	0.0	0.0	0.1	0.03
Celtis occidentalis	0.3	0.2	0.1	0.20
Circaea lutetiana ssp. canadensis	0.0	0.1	0.0	0.03
Crataegus sp.	0.0	0.0	0.1	0.03
Dioscorea villosa	0.0	0.1	0.0	0.03
Euonymus atropurpurea	0.0	0.1	0.2	0.10
Galium aparine	0.0	0.1	0.0	0.03
Geranium maculatum	0.2	0.0	0.1	0.10
Geum sp.	0.0	0.1	0.1	0.07
Hydrophyllum virginianum	0.2	0.0	0.1	0.10
Lonicera (exotic) sp.	0.1	0.7	0.2	0.33
Maianthemum canadense	0.2	0.2	0.3	0.23
Parthenocissus sp.	0.3	0.0	0.5	0.27
Prunus serotina	0.0	0.4	0.2	0.20
Prunus virginiana	0.1	0.0	0.1	0.07
Rhamnus cathartica	0.8	0.8	1	0.87
R bes cynosbati	0.0	0.1	0.3	0.13
R bes sp.	0.1	0.0	0.0	0.03
Sanguinaria canadensis	0.1	0.0	0.0	0.03
Smilax tamnoides	0.1	0.0	0.0	0.03
Solidago sp.	0.0	0.0	0.1	0.03
Streptopus lanceolatus var. roseus	0.0	0.1	0.0	0.03
Ulmus rubra	0.0	0.2	0.0	0.07
Viola sp.	0.0	0.0	0.1	0.03
Vitis riparia	0.2	0.0	0.0	0.07

Plot: 5084

Species	Quadrat Frequency Transect 1	2	3	Mean Quadrat Frequency
Arctium minus	0.0	0.4	1	0.47
Bromus inermis	0.0	0.0	0.6	0.20
Cardamine impatiens	0.0	0.0	0.2	0.07
Celtis occidentalis	0.0	0.1	0.1	0.07
Circaea lutetiana ssp. canadensis	0.0	0.0	0.1	0.03
Cirsium arvense	0.0	0.0	0.1	0.03
Daucus carota	0.0	0.0	0.2	0.07
Echinocystis lobata	0.0	0.0	0.3	0.10
Fraxinus pennsylvanica	0.0	0.1	0.1	0.07
Glechoma hederacea	0.0	0.1	0.3	0.13
Hesperis matronalis	0.0	0.0	0.2	0.07
Laportea canadensis	0.0	0.1	0.1	0.07
Leonurus cardiaca	0.0	0.0	0.1	0.03
Parthenocissus sp.	0.0	0.0	0.2	0.07
Pilea sp.	0.0	0.0	0.5	0.17
Poaceae fam.	0.0	0.1	0.0	0.03
Polygonatum pubescens	0.0	0.0	0.2	0.07
Rhamnus cathartica	0.0	0.1	0.1	0.07
Solidago sp.	0.0	0.0	0.1	0.03
Urtica dioica ssp. gracilis	0.0	0.0	0.3	0.10
Viola sp.	0.0	0.0	0.1	0.03
Vitis riparia	0.0	0.2	0.0	0.07

Plot: 5086

Species	Quadrat Frequency Transect 1	2	3	Mean Quadrat Frequency
Acer negundo	0.1	0.4	0.0	0.17
Acer saccharinum	0.0	0.1	0.0	0.03
Cryptotaenia canadensis	0.0	0.2	0.0	0.07
Fraxinus pennsylvanica	0.3	0.1	0.4	0.27
Hydrocotyle americana	0.0	0.4	0.0	0.13
Impatiens sp.	0.1	0.1	0.2	0.13
Lamiaceae fam.	0.4	0.0	0.0	0.13
Laportea canadensis	0.3	0.2	0.0	0.17
Poaceae fam.	0.0	0.4	0.0	0.13
Solidago sp.	0.1	0.2	0.1	0.13
Viola sp.	0.0	0.3	0.0	0.10
Vitis riparia	0.3	0.2	0.0	0.17

Plot: 5096

Species	Quadrat Frequency Transect 1	2	3	Mean Quadrat Frequency
Acer negundo	0.1	0.0	0.0	0.03
Alliaria petiolata	1	0.8	0.5	0.77
Amphicarpaea bracteata	0.5	0.2	0.0	0.23
Anemone quinquefolia	0.1	0.0	0.1	0.07
Arisaema triphyllum	0.2	0.0	0.0	0.07
Carex pensylvanica	0.2	0.0	0.0	0.07
Celtis occidentalis	0.4	0.1	0.1	0.20
Circaea lutetiana ssp. canadensis	0.9	0.6	0.3	0.60
Fraxinus pennsylvanica	0.3	0.0	0.0	0.10
Galium aparine	0.7	0.6	0.5	0.60
Galium asprellum	0.0	0.0	0.1	0.03
Galium trifidum	0.5	0.2	0.0	0.23
Geum sp.	0.9	0.1	0.0	0.33
Glechoma hederacea	0.0	0.2	0.0	0.07
Laportea canadensis	0.2	0.0	0.0	0.07
Leonurus cardiaca	0.5	0.0	0.0	0.17
Lonicera (exotic) sp.	0.1	0.1	0.0	0.07
Parthenocissus sp.	0.2	0.2	0.4	0.27
Pilea sp.	0.4	0.1	0.1	0.20
Prunus serotina	0.8	0.3	0.4	0.50
Prunus virginiana	0.4	0.4	0.4	0.40
Pyrola sp.	0.0	0.1	0.0	0.03
Quercus ellipsoidalis	0.2	0.0	0.0	0.07
Ranunculus abortivus	0.0	0.0	0.1	0.03
Rhamnus cathartica	1	0.9	0.9	0.93
Ribes hirtellum	1	0.9	0.9	0.93
Rubus idaeus ssp. strigosus	0.0	0.1	0.1	0.07
Rubus occidentalis	0.0	0.1	0.0	0.03
Rubus pensilvanicus	0.2	0.2	0.0	0.13
Solanum dulcamara	0.0	0.0	0.1	0.03
Solidago sp.	0.0	0.2	0.0	0.07
Toxicodendron rydbergii	0.1	0.0	0.0	0.03
Ulmus rubra	0.2	0.3	0.2	0.23
Urtica dioica ssp. gracilis	0.1	0.0	0.0	0.03
Viola sp.	0.4	0.1	0.2	0.23
Vitis riparia	0.2	0.0	0.1	0.10
Zanthoxylum americanum	0.0	0.0	0.1	0.03

Plot: 5097

| Species | Quadrat Frequency | | | Mean Quadrat Frequency |
| | Transect | | | |
	1	2	3	
Acer negundo	0.0	0.0	0.1	0.03
Acer saccharum	0.1	0.0	0.0	0.03
Actaea sp.	0.1	0.0	0.0	0.03
Anemone quinquefolia	0.0	0.1	0.0	0.03
Arisaema triphyllum	0.0	0.3	0.5	0.27
Carex projecta	0.0	0.0	0.1	0.03
Carex sp.	0.0	0.0	0.1	0.03
Carya cordiformis	0.1	0.0	0.0	0.03
Caulophyllum thalictroides	0.1	0.1	0.3	0.17
Celtis occidentalis	0.0	0.2	0.0	0.07
Cinna arundinacea	0.0	0.0	0.1	0.03
Circaea lutetiana ssp. canadensis	0.2	0.3	0.3	0.27
Fraxinus pennsylvanica	0.0	0.1	0.1	0.07
Galium aparine	0.1	0.3	0.3	0.23
Hydrophyllum virginianum	0.2	0.3	0.4	0.30
Impatiens sp.	0.5	0.4	0.3	0.40
Laportea canadensis	0.3	0.6	0.6	0.50
Maianthemum canadense	0.0	0.1	0.0	0.03
Maianthemum racemosum	0.1	0.1	0.5	0.23
Menispermum canadense	0.3	0.0	0.6	0.30
Parthenocissus sp.	0.0	0.0	0.2	0.07
Plantago major	0.0	0.0	0.1	0.03
Poa compressa	0.0	0.0	0.1	0.03
Prunus serotina	0.0	0.0	0.1	0.03
Prunus virginiana	0.2	0.1	0.0	0.10
Quercus rubra	0.1	0.2	0.0	0.10
R bes hirtellum	0.2	0.3	0.6	0.37
Sanguinaria canadensis	0.2	0.0	0.2	0.13
Smilax ecirrata	0.1	0.0	0.0	0.03
Smilax tamnoides	0.0	0.3	0.3	0.20
Solidago flexicaulis	0.0	0.0	0.3	0.10
Thalictrum dioicum	0.1	0.0	0.0	0.03
Uvularia grandiflora	0.0	0.1	0.1	0.07
Uvularia sessilifolia	0.1	0.0	0.0	0.03
Viola sp.	0.2	0.4	0.4	0.33
Vitis riparia	0.0	0.0	0.1	0.03

Plot: 5099

| Species | Quadrat Frequency | | | Mean Quadrat Frequency |
| | Transect | | | |
	1	2	3	
Alliaria petiolata	0.4	0.2	0.0	0.20
Amphicarpaea bracteata	0.2	0.0	0.0	0.07
Bidens frondosa	0.0	0.1	0.0	0.03
Boehmeria cylindrica	0.2	0.3	0.0	0.17
Calamagrostis canadensis	0.0	0.1	0.0	0.03
Calystegia sepium	0.0	0.2	0.0	0.07
Cardamine impatiens	0.1	0.0	0.0	0.03
Cryptotaenia canadensis	0.1	0.0	0.0	0.03
Glechoma hederacea	0.0	0.1	0.0	0.03
Impatiens sp.	0.4	0.2	0.0	0.20
Laportea canadensis	0.8	0.4	0.6	0.60
Matteuccia struthiopteris	0.1	0.0	0.0	0.03
Pilea sp.	0.0	0.3	0.0	0.10
Poaceae fam.	0.3	0.0	0.0	0.10
Rudbeckia laciniata	0.3	0.2	0.0	0.17
Sambucus nigra ssp. canadensis	0.2	0.0	0.0	0.07
Solidago sp.	0.0	0.1	0.0	0.03
Teucrium canadense	0.0	0.3	0.0	0.10
Urtica dioica ssp. gracilis	0.2	0.1	0.0	0.10
Vitis riparia	0.3	0.0	0.0	0.10

Plot: 5104

| Species | Quadrat Frequency | | | Mean Quadrat Frequency |
| | Transect | | | |
	1	2	3	
Acer negundo	0.1	0.1	0.0	0.07
Acer saccharinum	0.0	0.1	0.0	0.03
Alliaria petiolata	0.3	0.0	0.0	0.10
Arctium minus	0.7	0.1	0.0	0.27
Boehmeria cylindrica	0.0	0.1	0.0	0.03
Carex blanda	0.3	0.4	0.0	0.23
Celtis occidentalis	0.3	0.0	0.0	0.10
Circaea lutetiana ssp. canadensis	0.3	0.1	0.0	0.13
Fraxinus pennsylvanica	0.4	0.3	0.1	0.27
Galium trifidum	0.3	0.0	0.0	0.10
Impatiens sp.	0.7	0.2	0.1	0.33
Laportea canadensis	0.0	0.0	0.3	0.10
Lemna minor	0.0	0.0	0.1	0.03
Menispermum canadense	0.1	0.0	0.0	0.03
Oxalis stricta	0.0	0.0	0.1	0.03
Parthenocissus sp.	0.6	0.1	0.1	0.27
Phalaris arundinacea	0.9	0.8	0.1	0.60
Poaceae fam.	0.0	0.1	0.0	0.03
Rhamnus cathartica	0.6	0.1	0.0	0.23
Scutellaria sp.	0.1	0.0	0.0	0.03
Solidago sp.	0.1	0.1	0.0	0.07
Taraxacum officinale	0.1	0.0	0.0	0.03
Thalictrum thalictroides	0.4	0.1	0.0	0.17
Viola sp.	0.6	0.1	0.2	0.30
Vitis riparia	0.3	0.3	0.1	0.23

Plot: 5106

Species	Quadrat Frequency Transect 1	2	3	Mean Quadrat Frequency
Calystegia sepium	0.2	0.0	0.0	0.07
Fraxinus pennsylvanica	0.1	0.0	0.0	0.03
Laportea canadensis	0.5	0.6	0.0	0.37
Lemna minor	0.0	0.0	0.2	0.07
Pilea sp.	0.0	0.1	0.0	0.03
Rudbeckia laciniata	0.4	0.0	0.0	0.13
Scutellaria sp.	0.2	0.0	0.0	0.07
Stachys sp.	0.1	0.0	0.0	0.03
Ulmus rubra	0.1	0.0	0.0	0.03
Urtica dioica ssp. gracilis	0.1	0.0	0.0	0.03

Plot: 5111

Species	Quadrat Frequency Transect 1	2	3	Mean Quadrat Frequency
Carex sp.	0.0	0.0	0.2	0.07
Ceratophyllum demersum	0.0	0.1	0.0	0.03
Lamiaceae fam.	0.0	0.0	0.1	0.03
Lemna minor	0.0	0.5	0.3	0.27
Phalaris arundinacea	0.3	0.0	0.2	0.17
Rhamnus cathartica	0.0	0.1	0.0	0.03
Sparganium sp.	0.0	0.1	0.0	0.03
Urtica dioica ssp. gracilis	0.0	0.0	0.1	0.03

Plot: 5140

Species	Quadrat Frequency Transect 1	2	3	Mean Quadrat Frequency
Alliaria petiolata	0.5	0.4	0.6	0.50
Arisaema triphyllum	0.4	0.4	0.6	0.47
Brachyelytrum erectum	0.0	0.2	0.1	0.10
Cardamine pensylvanica	0.1	0.0	0.0	0.03
Carex blanda	0.0	0.1	0.5	0.20
Carex sp.	0.1	0.1	0.0	0.07
Circaea lutetiana ssp. canadensis	0.2	0.2	0.2	0.20
Cornus alternifolia	0.1	0.1	0.1	0.10
Euonymus atropurpurea	0.0	0.1	0.0	0.03
Galium aparine	0.1	0.0	0.2	0.10
Geum sp.	0.0	0.1	0.1	0.07
Hydrophyllum virginianum	0.4	0.5	0.5	0.47
Impatiens sp.	0.9	0.7	0.5	0.70
Laportea canadensis	1	0.8	0.9	0.90
Leonurus cardiaca	0.0	0.1	0.0	0.03
Maianthemum racemosum	0.0	0.1	0.1	0.07
Parthenocissus sp.	0.1	0.3	0.0	0.13
Phlox divaricata	0.1	0.0	0.0	0.03
Polygonatum biflorum	0.0	0.0	0.1	0.03
Ranunculus abortivus	0.1	0.0	0.0	0.03
Rhamnus cathartica	0.1	0.0	0.1	0.07
Sanguinaria canadensis	0.1	0.2	0.1	0.13
Smilax ecirrata	0.0	0.1	0.0	0.03
Smilax tamnoides	0.0	0.1	0.1	0.07
Thalictrum dasycarpum	0.0	0.1	0.0	0.03
Viburnum opulus var. americanum	0.0	0.0	0.1	0.03
Viola sp.	0.0	0.0	0.1	0.03

Plot: 5142

Species	Quadrat Frequency Transect 1	2	3	Mean Quadrat Frequency
Bidens sp.	0.2	0.0	0.0	0.07
Calystegia sepium	0.1	0.0	0.0	0.03
Hydrocotyle americana	0.2	0.0	0.0	0.07
Impatiens capensis	0.1	0.2	0.0	0.10
Laportea canadensis	0.6	0.7	0.6	0.63
Lemna minor	0.0	0.0	0.3	0.10
Phalaris arundinacea	0.2	0.2	0.0	0.13
Pilea pumila	0.1	0.2	0.0	0.10
Poa sp.	0.0	0.1	0.0	0.03
Ranunculus sp.	0.1	0.1	0.0	0.07
Rudbeckia laciniata	0.5	0.5	0.0	0.33
Solidago sp.	0.2	0.1	0.0	0.10
Ulmus rubra	0.1	0.0	0.0	0.03
Urtica dioica ssp. gracilis	0.2	0.0	0.0	0.07
Vitis riparia	0.1	0.0	0.0	0.03

Plot: 5148

Species	Quadrat Frequency Transect 1	2	3	Mean Quadrat Frequency
Acer saccharinum	0.0	0.0	0.1	0.03
Alliaria petiolata	0.8	0.3	0.1	0.40
Amphicarpaea bracteata	0.1	0.2	0.0	0.10
Arctium minus	0.7	0.1	0.0	0.27
Boehmeria cylindrica	0.1	0.0	0.0	0.03
Brachyelytrum erectum	0.0	0.1	0.0	0.03
Celtis occidentalis	0.1	0.0	0.0	0.03
Circaea lutetiana ssp. canadensis	0.4	0.1	0.4	0.30
Cirsium arvense	0.1	0.0	0.0	0.03
Fraxinus pennsylvanica	0.1	0.1	0.0	0.07
Geum aleppicum	0.3	0.0	0.0	0.10
Glechoma hederacea	0.0	0.1	0.0	0.03
Heracleum sphondylium ssp. montanum	0.1	0.0	0.0	0.03
Hydrophyllum virginianum	0.0	0.1	0.0	0.03
Impatiens sp.	0.2	0.7	0.3	0.40
Laportea canadensis	0.5	1	0.9	0.80
Lysimachia nummularia	0.1	0.0	0.0	0.03
Menispermum canadense	0.1	0.0	0.0	0.03
Parthenocissus sp.	0.2	0.4	0.0	0.20
Phalaris arundinacea	0.2	0.1	0.1	0.13
Pilea sp.	0.2	0.0	0.0	0.07
Rhamnus cathartica	0.4	0.0	0.0	0.13
Ribes americanum	0.0	0.1	0.0	0.03
Scutellaria sp.	0.3	0.0	0.0	0.10
Sicyos angulatus	0.2	0.1	0.3	0.20
Solidago sp.	0.7	0.1	0.1	0.30
Urtica dioica ssp. gracilis	0.1	0.0	0.0	0.03
Viola sp.	0.1	0.1	0.1	0.10
Vitis riparia	0.2	0.0	0.0	0.07

NPS 607/116665, August 2012